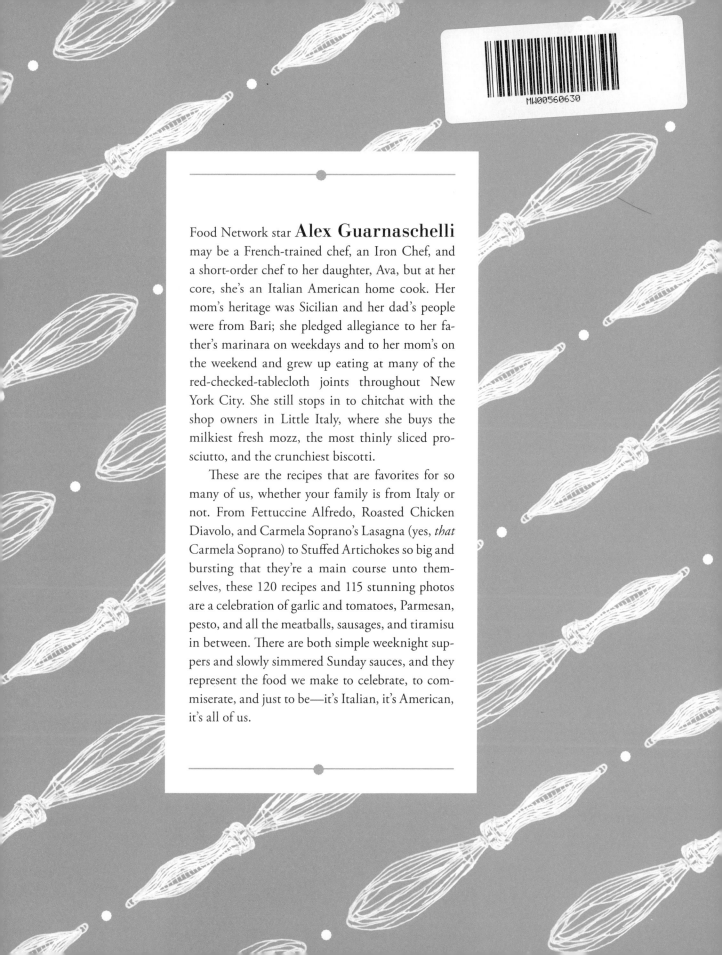

Food Network star **Alex Guarnaschelli** may be a French-trained chef, an Iron Chef, and a short-order chef to her daughter, Ava, but at her core, she's an Italian American home cook. Her mom's heritage was Sicilian and her dad's people were from Bari; she pledged allegiance to her father's marinara on weekdays and to her mom's on the weekend and grew up eating at many of the red-checked-tablecloth joints throughout New York City. She still stops in to chitchat with the shop owners in Little Italy, where she buys the milkiest fresh mozz, the most thinly sliced prosciutto, and the crunchiest biscotti.

These are the recipes that are favorites for so many of us, whether your family is from Italy or not. From Fettuccine Alfredo, Roasted Chicken Diavolo, and Carmela Soprano's Lasagna (yes, *that* Carmela Soprano) to Stuffed Artichokes so big and bursting that they're a main course unto themselves, these 120 recipes and 115 stunning photos are a celebration of garlic and tomatoes, Parmesan, pesto, and all the meatballs, sausages, and tiramisu in between. There are both simple weeknight suppers and slowly simmered Sunday sauces, and they represent the food we make to celebrate, to commiserate, and just to be—it's Italian, it's American, it's all of us.

ITALIAN AMERICAN FOREVER

Classic recipes for *everything* you want to eat

ITALIAN AMERICAN FOREVER

ALEX GUARNASCHELLI

PHOTOGRAPHS BY JOHNNY MILLER

CLARKSON POTTER/PUBLISHERS
New York

To my daughter,
sweet Ava Gruber
Simone Clark, and
Leon Duval Delele.
You are my only
forever family.

CONTENTS

The BAKERY

CLASSIC CAKES, ICE CREAM & DESSERTS

The CARDBOARD BOX TIED with the RED-and-WHITE STRING . . . & BEYOND

INTRODUCTION

●

Midtown Manhattan in the 1970s was not a culinary mecca.

On my block (Fifty-Fifth and Seventh Avenue) we *did* have the Carnegie Deli (Dad always got liverwurst sandwiches) and a bunch of quality coffee shops (where Mom ordered her grilled cheeses). I ate so many cheeseburgers growing up that my mother asked if I would ever care about food on any level . . . oh, the irony. At home, we cooked. A lot. Usually whatever protein was in excess and marked down that week at the store, like "London Broil" steaks (which could've been any number of beef cuts). My dad would heat a pan until it literally warped from the heat and the handle melted slightly. Then he would drop the steak in (without oil) and watch the pan turn every shade of gray to black. He would flip the steak and then open the front door to the hallway of our building as if it was a step in a recipe. Sometimes the smoke alarm for the whole floor would go off. Along with the steak, we ate frozen Birds Eye vegetables that my dad pains-takingly heated with sugar, salt, and pepper. Or his doctored (shredded) green beans. Or his gently warmed lima beans. I loved the starchiness of those beans. They enabled me to pick out the virtues of salt, pepper, and sugar early on. My dad would put Walter Cronkite on the black-and-white Sanyo TV with a broken antenna. My mom would breeze in with a stack of cookbook manuscripts, and we ate, silently, in four minutes flat. I was growing up American for all I knew. Except for one small thing.

My dad made tomato sauce as if he were auditioning to run the Pentagon. Canned tomato paste and canned tomatoes (never fresh), oregano, garlic *and* garlic powder, and tons of salt were in the mix. Onions. A generous dose of sugar. A quick simmer. "My sauce is better than Mom's, eh?" he would semi-ask and semi-tell me, nudging me with his elbow and stirring the sauce. "Yes, Dad, it's better, but don't tell her," I'd whisper diplomatically. The tomato sauce meant more to him than any other thing he cooked. We ate it on pasta, on meat, and even on rice. It permeated a lot of our dinners. It was the one thing I associated with being Italian.

On weekends when Mom had more time, she'd make "her" tomato sauce with grated carrot, onion, and garlic quick-cooked in olive oil, with canned tomatoes (again, never fresh) and salt. She'd let it simmer for a spare twenty minutes and then spoon it over the pasta. "I think your father puts too much tomato paste and sugar in his sauce," she'd mutter as the food processor whirred. "Don't you?" she would ask me. Murky waters. My mom's maiden name was DiBenedetto and my father's side was all named either Guarnaschelli or Spinicelli. I was surrounded by temperamental Italians. "Your mother is from Sicily . . . Calabrese," my neighbor Fran informed me with a sacred nod. Those words made my mom seem slightly more dangerous even though I had no idea what they meant. "Yes, Ma," I'd tell her gently, "your sauce has so much more flavor than Dad's." Truth is, I felt bad for her because I felt my mom really needed "the win."

Each of my parents' sauces became an expression of their personalities. My dad whipped up an umami bomb by tinkering with many ingredients and letting them slowly come together, while Mom went for the simplicity of the vegetables to thicken and flavor her comparatively straightforward and quick recipe. Her sauce tasted pleasantly grassy and slightly raw in the best way, while Dad's was vibrant, tomatoey, and acidic in the best way.

When we ate out, wandering a few blocks west to the many small restaurants that littered Hell's Kitchen on Ninth Avenue, it was exciting. We frequently ate volcanically hot ziti or overly ricotta-ed lasagna, and I loved those meals, too. I learned how much I value the baked-forever-in-an-extremely-hot-oven taste. I expanded my knowledge of red-sauce-joint dishes past what my parents shared, and it honestly is the biggest food memory I have from growing up. It made my parents emotional, too. One time, my dad got into a fistfight with about a dozen people over some cannoli in front of Ferrara bakery, and my mother would go to the other end of the Earth and spend money we didn't have on a single bottle of balsamic vinegar (the good stuff). When she bought a pricey one at Dean & DeLuca, my dad didn't speak to her for almost a week. Over a bottle of vinegar! My dad was prepared to die on that hill.

I think this book is a chef's expression of classic red sauce dishes that have always been an integral part of New York City culture and, therefore, my life growing up here. This book is an exploration of my heritage and, strangely, dishes I have rarely, if ever, cooked in a restaurant. They are the dishes we make again and again to perfect them. They are the dishes we eat again and again because we crave them endlessly. Suffice to say, this book is from my heart, but it's also likely already in yours. I almost called this book *Things People Always Want to Eat*. I'm hoping that you'll agree when you cook your way through it.

Alex with Lou Di Palo at Di Palo's in New York City.

MY ITALIAN AMERICAN PANTRY

I generally stick to the same brands when making a lot of these dishes. I shop at Di Palo's in NYC's Little Italy for a lot of them. Here is my unsponsored take on some frequently used favorites.

Flour

I like the Caputo brand for durum wheat semolina flour and for extra-fine double zero (00) flour. The flavor and texture of these flours are great for consistent results when making fresh pasta (semolina flour) and pizza (00 flour).

Balsamic Vinegar

True balsamic vinegar, which is produced uniquely in Modena, Italy, comes in a few different forms. Some vinegars are aged for a few years and some for longer. The longer the age, the sweeter and more developed the flavor and the thicker and more naturally syrupy the texture. There are many great vinegars, but my personal favorite balsamic comes from Giuseppe Giusti. I like the one with the white label called Gran Deposito.

Red Wine Vinegar

I am fond of Regina red wine vinegar because I grew up with it. For the fancier moments, I use Pommery brand.

Olive Oil

Olive oil varies from year to year. It's like trying to find a great wine and expecting it to be the same every year. All I can say is trial and error (with your budget in mind) will yield you an oil you like. Most of the standard supermarket brands are pretty good. Some label info to look out for:

Extra-virgin olive oil means the olives are crushed for their oil but not heated. It's considered the **first cold pressing** and is the best quality oil and should be saved for dressings or cooking a piece of fish.

After the first press, olives are heated and pressed again to maximize yield. This second (heated) pressing yields just **olive oil**. Check the labels. You will note the absence of words like "virgin" and "cold pressing."

Blended oil that mixes a neutral oil (like canola) and olive oil is good for high-heat searing of meats and fish or vegetables. I cook with cheaper olive oils (or blended oil) when I'm searing or making sauces and saving the more expensive oil for drizzling and finishing.

Store your oil in a cool, dark place. Don't keep cooking oil on top of the stove; it heats and cools along with your stove when you're cooking. When I know I won't use my oil for a few days, I refrigerate it. It's expensive! If it firms up in the fridge, let it sit out and come to room temperature; it should take thirty minutes, tops.

Dry Pasta

I like De Cecco. When I worked in Italy for a few weeks last year, I was in a fancy restaurant in Rome and they pulled out the boxes of De Cecco. It's a hearty, tasty brand that's affordable, too.

Canned Tomatoes and Tomato Paste

I like Cento brand canned tomatoes or any brand that uses San Marzano tomatoes. If it says San Marzano on the can, that's what it is! I do like some fancier tomato pastes; if you see the Maria Grammatico "Estratto di Pomodoro" brand, buy it—it's exceptional stuff.

Tomato Passata

Passata is just a less intense version of tomato paste. I like the standard brands like Cento and Pomì.

Polenta

I like Divella Polenta Toscano. I sometimes cheat and use Marsh Hen Mill Grits.

Arborio Rice for Risotto

I like the Campanini brand of Arborio rice. It's consistent, not too expensive, and cooks evenly. While Arborio is the most classic type of rice for risotto, you can also buy Campanini brand Carnaroli rice (which is slightly starchier) or Vialone Nano (which is sturdier).

Anchovies

For jarred anchovies in oil, I use Agostino Recca fillets of anchovies in oil. Consistent. Good oil. Tasty fish.

Nuts

For all nuts, I favor the quality of Bazzini for everything from pine nuts to hazelnuts. For Italian pistachios, try the Brontedolci brand.

Spices

I buy my spices in a few places. My two favorite sources are SOS Chefs and Penzeys; their spices, from oregano to black pepper to garlic powder, are tasty. You can find both brands online.

Salts

I use Diamond Crystal kosher salt for pasta water, braises, sauces, and most baking, and Maldon flaky sea salt for finishing touches on steaks, fish, and vegetables. When salt is called for in the recipes in this book, know I'm using Diamond Crystal.

MOST OF ALL, buy what you like and what is delicious to you. Don't worry about what anyone else says or thinks.

SPICY ITALIAN SAUSAGE CROSTINI
WITH ONION JAM page 21

ANTI
& First Courses

Antipasti are little finger foods or
bites that traditionally signal the start
of an Italian meal. They can often be
as simple as dishes of artichoke hearts,
charred peppers, roasted grapes, or
olives with herbs, with slices of bread
to put everything on. Some of the
dishes in this chapter are designed to
be more an Italian American version
of a first course, so you can vary what
you serve and cook. Of course, for the
simplest antipasti, a platter of cured
meats and cheeses can be the greatest
opener to any meal, and Italy has the
best of both. (Sorry, France.)

HERBY PECORINO ARANCINI page 38

ASTI

THREE-MEAT MINI MEATBALLS page 32

SPICY ITALIAN SAUSAGE CROSTINI
WITH ONION JAM

MAKES 16 TOASTS

Spicy Italian pork sausage has so much built-in flavor that it will make your snack taste like you cooked all day. I think it's a total umami bomb where the flavors of the meat and spices collide with the bread, making it addictive. Here I pair the sausage, tomatoes, and peppers with the sweet notes of onions and put it all on crunchy toast. The idea is to get the sausage grease into the mix so that no bit of flavor is left behind—I even toast the bread in the sausage drippings. This bite is great with a cold beer, dry sparkling wine, or non-alcoholic cider to cool the spice . . . make the jam ahead of time and keep in the fridge.

ONION JAM

- 2 tablespoons extra-virgin olive oil
- 2 medium yellow onions, halved and thinly sliced
- 2 teaspoons sugar
- Kosher salt and freshly ground black pepper
- 1 tablespoon balsamic vinegar

CROSTINI

- 5 medium (3 to 4 ounces each) spicy Italian pork sausages
- 3 to 4 tablespoons extra-virgin olive oil
- 16 fresh sage leaves (or more, for serving)
- 1 medium baguette, cut into 16 (½-inch-thick) rounds
- Kosher salt

MAKE THE ONION JAM: Heat a large skillet over medium heat. When the pan is good and hot, add the oil, then the onions and sugar. Season with salt and pepper and cook over medium heat, stirring occasionally, until they become tender, 15 to 20 minutes. Stir in the vinegar.

COOK THE SAUSAGE: Line a plate with a double layer of paper towels. On a flat surface, use a sharp knife to cut each sausage into five even rounds. If the meat loosens at all, place the sausage round on the board and flatten gently. Heat a large skillet over high heat and add 1 tablespoon of the olive oil. When the oil begins to smoke lightly, add half of the sausage in a single layer and brown on the first sides, 2 to 3 minutes. Use a metal spatula to flip them and brown on the second sides, another 3 to 4 minutes. Remove the sausage and drain on the towel. Add the sage leaves to the skillet and crisp them in the sausage grease until they turn dark green, 1 to 2 minutes per side, then remove and drain with the sausage. Repeat to brown the remaining sausage.

BROWN THE BREAD: Heat 2 tablespoons olive oil in the same skillet over medium heat. When it begins to smoke lightly, add the baguette rounds in a single layer (work in batches and add more oil if needed) and brown carefully on both sides, 5 to 6 minutes total. Remove from the pan and arrange on a serving platter.

ASSEMBLE AND SERVE: Sprinkle the bread with a pinch of salt and spoon an even layer of the onion jam over each. Top with one to two pieces of the sausage and one sage leaf. If you made extra fried sage leaves, put some on the bottom of a large platter for decoration, then set the toasts on top.

ROASTED GARLIC TOASTS

MAKES 16 TO 20 TOASTS

Splitting and roasting whole heads of garlic makes the garlic tender, mellow, and absolutely delicious. Scoop the roasted garlic cloves out of their little homes using a small spoon or tip of a paring knife, then sprinkle with Maldon salt and eat them as is (they taste sweet like candy). Or take it one step further and pan-fry the roasted cloves in hot oil so they develop a crispy exterior but are still tender and sweet inside. For these toasts, I do both. The best thing you can add to the garlic? It's garlic powder, which adds that special pizzeria flavor that makes this toast so crave-able and such a great meal opener that only makes you hungrier . . .

4 large heads of garlic, halved horizontally through the middle

7 tablespoons extra-virgin olive oil

Maldon salt

3 teaspoons garlic powder

1 medium baguette, cut into 16 to 20 (½-inch) rounds

1 tablespoon balsamic vinegar

2 teaspoons honey

Preheat the oven to 350°F.

ROAST THE GARLIC: Arrange the garlic bottoms in a single layer on a sheet of tinfoil large enough to fold back over the garlic. Drizzle with 4 tablespoons of the olive oil and sprinkle with salt. Top with the other halves so they look like four heads of whole garlic. Fold the foil over the garlic, press tightly around the heads, and crimp the edges to seal. Place the foil package in the oven and bake until the garlic is completely tender when pierced with the tip of a knife, about 1 hour. Carefully open the foil and cool slightly.

CRISP HALF OF THE GARLIC: Once the garlic is cool enough to handle, use a small spoon or paring knife to scoop out the garlic cloves from the skins. Heat a medium skillet over medium heat. Add 1 tablespoon of the olive oil. When the oil begins to smoke lightly, remove the pan from the heat and sprinkle about half of the cloves into the oil in a single layer. Return the pan to the heat, shut off the heat, and cook the garlic in the residual heat, turning the cloves so they don't become overly brown. You want a crisp exterior that's light to golden brown, which should take 1 to 2 minutes. Remove the cloves as they become light brown. The smaller ones will cook more quickly. Season with salt and 1½ teaspoons of the garlic powder and set aside.

BROWN THE BREAD: In the same skillet, heat the remaining 2 tablespoons olive oil over medium heat. When it begins to smoke lightly, add the baguette rounds in a single layer (working in batches if needed and adding more oil if the pan becomes dry) and brown for 2 to 3 minutes on each side. Remove from the pan and arrange directly on a serving platter.

ASSEMBLE AND SERVE: In a medium bowl, gently crush the remaining roasted garlic cloves with the back of a spoon. Season with salt and add the remaining 1½ teaspoons garlic powder, the balsamic vinegar, and honey. Sprinkle the bread with a pinch of salt, spoon an even layer of the garlic mix over each, and top with the crisped garlic cloves.

MY FAVORITE SALAMI & CHEESE BOARDS

It's no secret that I am all about Di Palo's on Grand Street in Manhattan's Little Italy, my original Italian ingredient mecca from childhood. Whether you shop at Eataly or any Italian specialty grocer, you must source the best ingredients possible for a charcuterie and cheese moment. What I serve on that board is forever evolving and changing . . .

I have many friends who don't eat meat and so I now make two boards, one with the cheese and condiments and the other with the meat—and the two never mix.

MY TRIFECTA OF FAVORITE MEATS:

THE HEAT
Spicy Soppressata

Soppressata is a cured pork sausage made in many regions of southern Italy. I like the ones made traditionally with hints of chile peppers, peppercorns, and even cinnamon. The nitty gritty: Soppressata is made by coarsely grinding pork belly, leaving big pieces of fat and meat, which give the final product a rich and addictive taste.

THE SALTY
Prosciutto di Parma

Imported prosciutto di Parma is my favorite. It's a giant cured and dried pork leg that's rich and nutty but also salty.

THE RICH AND SPICED
Mortadella

Mortadella is a sausage (like lunch meat) made of finely ground pork mixed with pork fat. More modern versions are studded with pistachios, which I love for the added texture. It has nutmeg and warm spice notes and reminds me, in the best way, of bologna. It's tasty parked next to spicy salami.

MY TRIFECTA OF FAVORITE CHEESES:

THE CREAMY AND SPREADABLE
Fresh Ricotta

Ricotta is a fresh Italian cheese made from any variety of milk: sheep, cow, or goat, or buffalo milk whey (which is left over from cheese making). I love to stir in some lemon zest or fresh thyme to amplify the creamy notes of ricotta without obscuring its sweetness.

THE FRESH AND OOZY
Burrata

Burrata is a fresh Italian cow's milk (or occasionally buffalo milk) cheese made from mozzarella that is finished with cream instead of milk. The added fat from the cream makes it richer and looser in texture. This is a creamy cheese that plays so nicely with condiments.

THE SHARP
Gorgonzola

Gorgonzola is a soft, blue, buttery cheese made from raw cow's milk. The tangy blue cheese is a welcome companion to the creamy and sweet cheese already here. There is also Gorgonzola dolce, but I like the saltiness of regular Gorgonzola here.

MY TRIFECTA OF CONDIMENTS AND COMPANIONS:

Olives

Castelvetrano or Cerignola (green) olives are my favorite. I simply toss with some red pepper flakes and lemon zest. If you serve unpitted olives, remember to set out a small dish for pits.

Honey

I love a truffled honey or chestnut honey to go with both the cheeses and meats. My mother used to put out a wedge of a straight (and gloriously waxy) honeycomb with a spoon, which I also love.

Grainy Mustard

Mustard of some kind is a must, and I love the pop of the seeds from grainy mustard for texture against the soft cheeses and salty meats.

Fresh and Dried Fruits and Fresh Vegetables

I like adding fresh vegetables or fruits (cherry tomatoes, thinly sliced celery, carrot matchsticks, seedless grapes, or cherries) because they add freshness to complement all the bold, hearty flavors.

You Must Have Bread

A friend recently told me, "No one eats bread anymore." Um. Wrong.

Serve thinly sliced baguette or slices of toasted sourdough. Some crackers made with rosemary or dried fruits are lovely, too. Don't forget pretzel sticks—their salty and browned flavor notes and crunchy texture are great with the cured meats and cheeses.

Serving

When making your platters, think of yourself as a curator in an art museum. What paintings will speak to each other or benefit from being nearby? As an example, I arrange the thin slices of salami and mortadella in rows, then park olives and a pot of mustard near the meat so people know to group those flavors.

I arrange the cheeses and honey on the other board. I might add a bowl of pickle slices or other pickled vegetables like caper berries. Salty companions bring out the nutty and creamy notes in the cheese. A jar of jam or marmalade is a fun addition, too.

STUFFED TOMATOES
WITH PEAS & PECORINO

●

MAKES 24

A chef's best-kept secret (or one of them, at least) is that the best spring and summer peas are often from the freezer section of the supermarket. Here, I count on their starchy sweet notes, which are reminiscent of a fresh fava bean (with far less work), to play nicely with the tartness of tomatoes and the saltiness of pecorino. I make the one-bite stuffed tomatoes in advance and serve them straight from the refrigerator. They are elegant and, really, sometimes it's nice to offer a snack that doesn't involve bread.

24 medium cherry tomatoes

3 tablespoons extra-virgin olive oil

3 scallions (green and white parts), coarsely chopped

1 large garlic clove, grated

1 teaspoon garlic powder

1 teaspoon honey

6 ounces frozen peas, thawed

3 sprigs fresh basil, stemmed and coarsely chopped

2 teaspoons red wine vinegar

⅓ cup finely grated pecorino cheese

Kosher salt

Fresh herb sprigs, such as basil, for serving (optional)

PREP THE TOMATOES: Cut off the top one-fourth of a tomato and reserve the "hat," then cut a little off the bottom so the tomato sits upright on a flat surface without rolling around. Use the handle of a small spoon to scoop out the insides into a small bowl, placing the hollowed tomato back on the flat surface. Repeat with all the tomatoes.

MAKE THE FILLING: In a large, heavy-bottomed pot, heat the olive oil over medium heat. When the oil begins to smoke lightly, add the scallions, garlic, garlic powder, honey, and reserved insides of the tomatoes. Season with salt and cook over high heat, stirring with a wooden spoon, until the scallions are tender, 3 to 5 minutes. Stir in the peas and basil. Season with vinegar, add the cheese, and stir to combine. Taste for seasoning.

ASSEMBLE AND SERVE: Sprinkle the insides of the tomatoes with salt. Spoon the filling liberally into each tomato and top with its tomato hat. Place a few herb sprigs on a platter—these help keep the tomatoes from rolling around—and set the tomatoes on top.

GNOCCHI ALLA ROMANA

SERVES 4 TO 6 (28 TO 32 PIECES)

This is just gnocchi made simpler by subbing in semolina flour (my favorite is Caputo brand) for the riced potatoes of the classic version. The resulting dish resembles a cheesy version of a potato gratin. For years, I thought that semolina was made from some type of corn flour because of its yellow color. Come to discover, it's actually made from durum wheat. This gnocchi does resemble firm polenta but has the flavor of the wheat. These are not traditionally shaped gnocchi you would see made from potatoes. These "gnocchi" are actually more like thickly sliced rounds. It makes a simpler, more humble gnocchi. Sage adds an earthy, almost minty taste and the butter and salty cheeses offer a playful richness, leaving plenty of room for the gnocchi to play in the appetizer space as a hearty opener to a meal. This also works as a side for braised meats or even shellfish or a fish soup.

2 cups whole milk	½ cup semolina flour
6 tablespoons (¾ stick) unsalted butter	1 cup finely grated Parmesan cheese
¼ teaspoon ground allspice	2 large egg yolks
Kosher salt	12 to 16 fresh sage leaves

MAKE THE GNOCCHI DOUGH: In a large, heavy-bottomed skillet, heat the milk and 2 tablespoons of the butter over medium heat with the allspice and a generous pinch of salt. When it begins to simmer, remove from the heat and vigorously whisk in the semolina so no lumps form. Return the mixture to medium heat and cook until it thickens, still whisking, 2 to 3 minutes. Stir in a generous half of the Parmesan cheese. Add an egg yolk and stir until combined. The mixture almost looks like a cookie dough.

FORM THE GNOCCHI: Prepare a medium bowl of cool water with a few ice cubes to cool your hands as you work. Line two baking sheets with parchment paper and spoon half the mix (the long way) onto each piece of parchment, creating strips as even in width as possible and leaving a 2-inch gap at the bottom. Working one at a time, roll the parchment around the dough to shape it into a log. Dip your hands in the cool water if they get hot while you are rolling up the log. Refrigerate the logs for about 1 hour, or until the semolina is firm and chilled.

Preheat the oven to 375°F. Position a rack in the center of the oven.

COOK THE SAGE: In a medium pan over medium heat, melt the remaining butter with the sage leaves, simmering gently so the sage wilts and loses some of its medicinal flavor, about 2 minutes. Transfer the sage to doubled paper towels, turn off the heat, and set both the sage and the sage butter aside.

SLICE THE GNOCCHI: Brush the bottom and sides of an 8 × 13-inch baking dish with some of the melted sage butter. Unwrap the logs of gnocchi. On a flat surface and using a wet knife (to help make even cuts), slice each log into ¼-inch-thick rounds. Arrange the rounds, slightly overlapping, in rows in the baking dish.

BAKE AND SERVE: Whisk the remaining egg yolk in a small bowl and use a pastry brush to lightly coat the gnocchi. Pour the remaining sage butter over the gnocchi and sprinkle with the remaining cheese. Place the dish on the center rack and bake until browned, 18 to 20 minutes. If desired, place the gnocchi under the broiler and broil until lightly browned on top, 1 to 2 minutes. Top with the reserved crisped sage. Place the hot dish right in the center of the table and let people serve themselves, family style.

ANTIPASTI & FIRST COURSES

ONION FLANS
WITH CHEESY PECORINO FONDUTA

SERVES 6

Think of this as an Italian version of a crustless quiche served with a fonduta, the fancy-pants word for a cheesy sauce, made with any combination of cheese, milk, eggs, and butter, that is often flavored with fresh truffles. I use pecorino here because it's super salty and earthy. This is a simple recipe and the ingredients go so well together. Serve with a super vinegary salad of bitter greens or some juicy tomatoes drizzled with balsamic. The toasted walnuts and scallions add some needed crunch and an oniony "bite" to the dish. Don't limit this to the appetizer category. I have served this as a main course with a few salads and vegetables.

FLAN

2 tablespoons unsalted butter

2 large yellow onions, halved and thinly sliced

Kosher salt and freshly ground black pepper

4 large eggs

1 cup whole milk

1 cup heavy cream

FONDUTA

½ cup heavy cream

1 cup finely grated pecorino cheese

1 teaspoon Worcestershire sauce

Ground nutmeg

GARNISHES

2 scallions (green and white parts), thinly sliced

¼ cup walnuts, lightly crushed and toasted

Maldon salt

COOK THE ONIONS: In a large skillet, melt the butter over medium heat. Add the onions, season with kosher salt and pepper, and cook, stirring occasionally, until the onions become tender and browned, 12 to 15 minutes. Taste for seasoning. Set aside to cool.

MAKE THE FLAN CUSTARD: In a medium bowl, whisk the eggs to break them up. In a medium pot over medium heat, combine the milk and cream and bring to a simmer, 2 to 3 minutes. Pour a little cream mix over the eggs and whisk to temper the eggs. Add all of the milk mix to the eggs, and then pour it back into the pot. Cook *gently*, whisking constantly, until thicker, 3 to 5 minutes. Transfer the custard to another medium bowl to cool.

Preheat the oven to 275°F. Position a rack in the center of the oven.

ASSEMBLE: Arrange six 6-ounce ramekins (3-inch diameter) in a baking pan with high sides. Line the bottom of each ramekin with a layer of the cooked onions and gently pour the flan mix over the onions almost to the top. Pour about 1 inch of warm water in the bottom of the pan to create steam as the flans cook. Cover the whole pan tightly with foil to seal in the steam. Gently place the pan in the center rack of the oven and cook until firmed up but still slightly loose and jiggly in the center, 50 to 55 minutes. Remove from the oven and carefully remove the foil. Remove the ramekins from the water bath and set aside to cool slightly for about 30 minutes.

MAKE THE FONDUTA: In a small pot, warm the cream over medium heat until it simmers gently. Turn off the heat and add the pecorino, Worcestershire, and a tiny pinch of nutmeg. Let it sit in the pot and steep for 8 to 10 minutes. Stir so the cheese blends with the cream.

SERVE: After the flans cool, run a paring knife around the top edge of each ramekin to loosen it and unmold the custard onto a plate. Spoon fonduta over the top of each and top with the scallions, walnuts, and a tiny pinch of Maldon salt.

PS: If your cheese sauce looks grainy, stir in a splash of warm water. It's usually too much fat that creates problems and a little water can often balance that out.

THREE-MEAT MINI MEATBALLS

MAKES 32 TO 34 MINI MEATBALLS

My seven rules for meatballs never change:

1. Don't overmix the meat unless you want tough meatballs.

2. Make a small patty and brown in a pan, then taste for seasoning *before* rolling and cooking the whole batch.

3. Curly parsley was made for meatballs; don't sleep on it.

4. Meatballs taste better after they cool and sit in the sauce overnight.

5. Make double what you think you need.

6. The better the meat, the better the meatball.

7. Cook meatballs like hamburgers—medium-rare—then, gently finish in the sauce.

SAUCE

3 tablespoons extra-virgin olive oil

2 medium yellow onions, halved and thinly sliced

5 large garlic cloves, thinly sliced

Kosher salt

1 (28-ounce) can peeled whole tomatoes with their juices

1 teaspoon sugar

1 teaspoon dried oregano

MEATBALLS

½ pound (8 ounces) ground beef (85% lean)

½ pound (8 ounces) ground veal

½ pound (8 ounces) ground pork

(meatballs continued)

1 cup finely grated Parmesan cheese

12 sprigs fresh curly parsley (stems and all), chopped

½ cup panko breadcrumbs

1 large egg, lightly beaten

Kosher salt

1 tablespoon garlic powder

1 teaspoon dried oregano

¼ teaspoon red pepper flakes

3 to 4 tablespoons extra-virgin olive oil

TO FINISH

½ cup fresh basil leaves

½ cup finely grated Parmesan cheese

Bread, for serving (optional)

MAKE THE SAUCE: In a large skillet, heat the olive oil. Add the onion and garlic and a generous sprinkle of salt to start. Cook, stirring from time to time with a wooden spoon, until the onions are translucent, 3 to 4 minutes. Add the canned tomatoes, sugar, and oregano and simmer over medium heat, stirring from time to time, until the metallic note from the tomatoes fades and the sweetness sets in, 10 to 12 minutes. Taste for seasoning. Keep warm.

MAKE THE MEATBALL MIX: Spread the beef, veal, and pork across the bottom and sides of a large bowl, interspersing them so you are mixing the meats without using your hands. Sprinkle with the Parmesan, parsley, breadcrumbs, egg, 1 tablespoon salt, garlic powder, oregano, and red pepper flakes and gently mix with your hands only until combined. Roll into balls about 1 inch in diameter (you should get 32 to 34 mini meatballs).

BROWN THE MEATBALLS: Heat 3 tablespoons of the olive oil in a large skillet over high heat. When the oil begins to smoke lightly, shut off the heat (to avoid splattering). Add half of the meatballs in a single layer and spread somewhat apart so they have a chance to brown instead of steaming. Put the heat back on high and cook, turning the meatballs so they brown all around, 3 to 5 minutes total. Treat them like hamburgers and cook them until they are medium-rare (I like to press them lightly in the middle starting at the 2½ minute mark, to make sure they give a little so I don't let them cook past medium-rare). Use a slotted spoon or spatula to transfer to a baking sheet to cool. Repeat with the remaining meatballs and additional oil if needed.

FINISH: Add the meatballs to the sauce and allow them to bubble slightly over very low heat, until hot in the center, 12 to 15 minutes. Best way to know? Taste one! Stir the basil and remaining cheese into the sauce. Serve hot with toothpicks and bread on the side if you like.

MORTADELLA FINGER SANDWICHES
WITH TUSCAN RELISH

MAKES 8 SANDWICHES

I spent a month in Tuscany last summer and somehow ended up feeling homesick for the taste of pickles. But it makes sense because the salty sweet taste pairs brilliantly with so many Tuscan ingredients—mortadella, balsamic, and Parmigiano Reggiano cheese, for example. When I got home to New York, I went down to Little Italy and had some mortadella from Di Palo's. Wow. Now, mortadella is like that famous American lunchmeat with a wonderful rich taste. I came home with some, studded with pistachios, and made a chopped pickle relish with the classic Tuscan flavors of kale and green olives tinged with balsamic. It is so tasty with the richness of the mortadella. Cut to make eight finger sandwiches, or cut in half again to make sixteen smaller square sandwiches.

RELISH

3 leaves Tuscan kale (stems and all), very finely minced

2 tablespoons extra-virgin olive oil

Kosher salt

½ cup green Castelvetrano or Cerignola olives, pitted and coarsely chopped

2 tablespoons roughly chopped dill pickle

1 tablespoon balsamic vinegar

SANDWICHES

8 square slices sourdough bread

4 thin slices provolone cheese

Maldon salt

½ teaspoon sweet paprika

20 thin slices mortadella, rolled into tubes

MAKE THE RELISH: In a medium bowl, "massage" the kale with the oil and a pinch of kosher salt. The oil soaking into the kale will tenderize it. Let rest for 10 minutes. Mix in the olives, pickles, and balsamic, mashing them together with the back of a spoon, and refrigerate for at least 1 hour or up to 3 days.

ASSEMBLE: Place four slices of the bread on a flat surface and arrange one slice of provolone on each slice of bread. Sprinkle with Maldon salt and use a small strainer to "sift" an even layer of paprika over the cheese. Place five mortadella tubes in a row on top of the cheese on each piece of bread. Spoon an even layer of the relish down the length of each. Press the other four slices of bread on top to make four sandwiches. Using a serrated knife, cut each sandwich in half. Serve with more relish on the tops or on the side.

ROASTED GRAPES
WITH GORGONZOLA

SERVES 4 TO 6

I like to use seedless grapes because the uninterrupted texture from the bursting of the fruit in your mouth is *so* good. That said, deeply flavored Concord grapes (yes, they often have seeds, but you can find seedless Concords now) are incredibly delicious, too. Gorgonzola dolce is both sweet and tangy from the blue notes, but if you don't like the dolce, use classic Gorgonzola instead. It's slightly sharper, saltier, and certainly less naturally sweet and creamy. Serve the grapes with anything from classic Chianti to a gin martini, or even just a glass of tonic water over ice with a wedge of lemon.

2 tablespoons extra-virgin olive oil

1 tablespoon honey

2 teaspoons Maldon salt

1 teaspoon freshly ground black pepper

3 cups seedless red grapes, stems removed and reserved

8 ounces Gorgonzola dolce

Preheat the oven to 375°F. Line a baking sheet with foil.

ROAST THE GRAPES: In a large bowl, whisk together the olive oil, honey, salt, and pepper. Toss the grapes in the bowl to coat them with the oil mix. Arrange the grapes in a single layer on the baking sheet and roast until somewhat tender, 10 to 12 minutes. Set aside to cool.

ASSEMBLE: Spoon a little of the cheese on each grape and spear with toothpicks for easy eating. Arrange the reserved stems on a platter and nestle the grapes over them. The stems act like a cage that perfectly supports the grapes.

HERBY PECORINO ARANCINI

●

MAKES 24 OR 48 ARANCINI, DEPENDING ON SIZE

Arancini comes from the Italian word for "orange" because the Sicilian treat resembles an orange in shape. These arancini are all about carefully layering flavors—the shallots, the wine, and the punchy pecorino—and giving each one its moment alone with the rice before adding another (you're essentially making risotto that will be breaded and fried). Be patient. (Have you ever tasted uncooked rice? Ruins the mood.) While many cooks make risotto with chicken stock (or any stock), I am partial to water since it allows other flavors to stand out, like the starchy, nutty flavors of the rice against the salty and creamy notes of the cheese. Flavorful stocks interrupt that purity. (My rule is, if there is no chicken in the dish, why use chicken stock?) For the herbs, I enlist curly parsley, which incidentally is, in my opinion, the only parsley to use for meatballs, for an extra grassy note. You need that grassy punch against all the cheese and the rice itself.

2 tablespoons extra-virgin olive oil

2½ cups (1 pound) Arborio rice

Maldon salt

4 medium shallots, minced

½ cup dry white wine

2 cups finely grated pecorino cheese

1 cup (8 ounces) mascarpone cheese

14 sprigs fresh curly parsley (stems and all), finely chopped

6 sprigs fresh basil (stems and all), finely chopped

2 large eggs, lightly beaten

2 cups panko breadcrumbs

Canola or avocado oil, for frying

2 to 3 tablespoons aged balsamic vinegar

TOAST THE RICE: Line a baking sheet with parchment paper. Heat about 2 quarts water in a medium pot. In a large sauté pan over medium heat, add the olive oil and rice and season with salt. Using a wooden spoon, stir to coat the rice with the oil and then smooth it gently into a uniform layer. Then listen for the sound of the rice popping and smell the rice getting nutty; it should take 2 to 3 minutes. Stir the rice, moving it around so another layer toasts gently, and toast for an additional 1 to 2 minutes.

COOK THE RICE: Stir in the shallots with a pinch of salt and cook, stirring with a wooden spoon, until the shallots are translucent, 2 to 3 minutes. Add the white wine and cook, stirring constantly, until the wine evaporates. Ladle in enough hot water just to cover the rice. Simmer, uncovered and stirring constantly, until the rice has absorbed a fair amount of the liquid.

FINISH THE RICE: From this point, the rice should take 16 to 20 minutes to cook: Add the water in small increments, cooking and stirring until it has been absorbed before adding the next ladleful. Cook until the rice is tender but still has a firm "bite," like pasta cooked al dente. Shut off the heat and stir the pecorino into the rice. Let it sit on the stove for 5 to 8 minutes to cool and thicken slightly. Taste for seasoning. Stir in the mascarpone, parsley, and basil. Spread the risotto on the prepared baking sheet and refrigerate until completely chilled, 4 to 6 hours.

ROLL THE BALLS: Form the chilled rice into larger balls (1½ to 2 inches in diameter) or smaller balls (¾ to 1 inch in diameter) and refrigerate again for at least 2 hours to firm up. Put the beaten eggs in a shallow dish and spread the panko in another. Roll the rice balls in the egg to coat and then in the breadcrumbs. At this point, you can freeze the arancini to fry in small batches whenever you like.

FRY THE BALLS: Pour the canola oil into a medium, heavy-bottomed pot. Heat the oil over medium heat to 350°F. Prepare a baking sheet fitted with a kitchen towel and a slotted spoon. If necessary, preheat the oven to 300°F to keep the arancini warm after frying.

Drop half of the risotto balls into the oil and gently swirl the oil as they fry. Swirling will assure the balls fry evenly on all sides. When they are light to medium brown all over, 3 to 5 minutes, remove them with a slotted spoon and place on doubled paper towels to drain. Season immediately with salt. Fry the remaining ones, keeping the first batch warm in the oven for 10 to 15 minutes if need be. *Note*: If you fry the arancini from frozen, which is fine, warm them in the oven after frying for a few additional minutes to assure they are hot in the center. Otherwise, serve immediately.

ROASTED GARLIC TOASTS page 22

SALADS

CHOPPED SALAD THAT COULD
DOUBLE AS AN ITALIAN DELI SANDWICH
page 51

SOUPS

One of my favorite things in the world is iceberg lettuce so cold from the refrigerator that it's almost frozen and splashed with tons of red wine vinegar and dried oregano. It takes me straight to an NYC slice joint. Some of these salads are those pizzeria classics: escarole, Caesar, and even a tasty caprese. To me, these salads never go out of style. I've also added a few of my favorite soups, which always inspire big food core memories from my childhood— like my mother ladling me a hot bowl of minestrone right at the stove.

QUICK CAESAR SALAD

●

SERVES 2 TO 4

As far as Caesar dressing goes, I'm a fan of the classic . . . sort of. I don't add an egg yolk because it can actually be chalky-tasting and can freak people out. With the absence of the rich yolk, the flavor of the anchovy becomes especially important (even if you are just using a little oil that the anchovies are packed in). In a pinch, I've also used the liquid from a can of tuna packed in oil to flavor this dressing in place of the anchovy, then crumbled the tuna over the lettuce for a little extra heft. I definitely recommend making the dressing in advance (it can be stored, refrigerated, for up to 2 days) and keeping it in the door of the fridge so you have some ready for a Caesar fix. Toss the dressing with the lettuce at the very last second.

DRESSING

1 tablespoon smooth Dijon mustard

2 large garlic cloves, grated

Kosher salt and coarsely ground black pepper

Juice from 2 large lemons

1 tablespoon brine from jarred capers or pickles

6 tablespoons extra-virgin olive oil

4 anchovy fillets, finely chopped, plus 2 teaspoons of the anchovy oil

CROUTONS

2 tablespoons extra-virgin olive oil

3 (1½-inch-thick) slices sourdough bread, cubed

¼ teaspoon hot paprika

¼ cup finely grated Parmesan cheese

SALAD

3 medium heads of romaine lettuce, outer layer discarded, leaves cut into 1-inch pieces

Chunk of Parmesan cheese, for grating or shaving

MAKE THE DRESSING: In the bowl of a food processor, combine the mustard, garlic, a pinch of salt, and about 1 teaspoon pepper. Pulse to blend. With the machine running, pour the lemon juice and caper brine into the mix. Then slowly pour in the olive oil. Transfer the dressing to a bowl. Taste for seasoning. Too lemony? Add more oil. Too oily? Add more lemon. Stir in the anchovies and anchovy oil. Refrigerate.

MAKE THE CROUTONS: Line a plate with a clean kitchen towel. Heat a large skillet over medium heat. Add the olive oil, then the bread cubes, and sprinkle with the paprika. Cook, tossing often and reducing the heat to low if needed, until they become brown and feel crispy to the touch, 3 to 5 minutes. Use a slotted spoon or spatula to transfer the croutons from the pan to drain on the kitchen towel. Sprinkle with the Parmesan cheese.

ASSEMBLE THE SALAD: In a large bowl, add the lettuce and grate a generous amount of cheese over all of it. Add about three-quarters of the dressing and gently toss the romaine with the dressing. Grate or shave Parmesan over the salad and serve.

PS: If your dressing doesn't come together, whisk in a splash of warm water.

ESCAROLE & APPLES
WITH CAPERS & ANCHOVIES

SERVES 4 TO 6; MAKES ¾ CUP VINAIGRETTE

Escarole can be bitter, like radicchio or endive, and is best served torn into smaller pieces so it offers a tender bite when mixed with other salad ingredients—perhaps crisp sweet apple or pear, or celery. Capers are transformed once they've been tempered by a few minutes of pan-frying: They become crispy and lose their intense saltiness, too. Cornichons, on the other hand, are a wonderful source of acidity and crunch. I hardly ever salt a salad because the vinegar and other ingredients in the dressing and salad bring a complex and vibrant enough flavor to skip basic seasoning—especially for a salad like this, where the capers and pickles add a nice amount of salt on their own. So wait until just before serving to taste and then grab the salt shaker.

DRESSING

4 tablespoons extra-virgin olive oil

2 tablespoons capers, drained

1 large shallot, finely diced

4 anchovy fillets

Juice from 2 large lemons (about ¼ cup)

1 tablespoon smooth Dijon mustard

6 small cornichons, thinly sliced

Kosher salt and fresh black pepper, if needed

SALAD

2 large heads of escarole (about 1½ pounds total), trimmed, leaves torn into bite-size pieces

1 Fuji or Cameo apple, cored and thinly sliced

FRY THE CAPERS: In a small skillet, heat 2 tablespoons of the olive oil over medium heat and add the capers. Cook until the capers bubble and become crispy, 3 to 5 minutes. Stir in the shallot and cook for 1 minute to soften.

MAKE THE DRESSING: Transfer the caper mixture to a medium bowl and add the anchovies. Press the anchovies against the bowl with the back of a spoon to break them up. Whisk in the remaining 2 tablespoons olive oil, the lemon juice, mustard, and cornichons. Taste for seasoning.

ASSEMBLE THE SALAD: In a large bowl, gently toss the escarole with the dressing. Sprinkle with the apple slices. Taste for seasoning and serve.

BROOKLYN ICEBERG
WITH RED WINE DRESSING

SERVES 4 TO 6

This is a pizzeria salad. My most memorable version was served at the famed Lucali pizzeria in Brooklyn. As a young adult, I looked to this salad as the perfect excuse to turn a few slices of pizza and garlic knots into a "healthy" meal. Can you make this salad with expensive olives, shallots, and cheffy lamb's lettuce? Sure. But we are going for an effect here. A nostalgic one, where the metallic notes from the canned olives are appreciated against the bracing acidity of red wine vinegar. If you want, use fancy-pants olives like pitted Castelvetrano or Cerignola; but to me, canned black olives are gloriously nostalgic and pleasantly tinny. If you want the full Brooklyn effect, the lettuce must be cold from the fridge and the dressing dropped on last minute.

SALAD

1 small red onion, halved and thinly sliced

2 large heads of iceberg lettuce, outer layer discarded, halved and pulled apart

1 medium cucumber, peeled and cut into thin rounds

1 cup cherry tomatoes, stemmed

1 cup canned black olives, drained

2 teaspoons oregano

VINAIGRETTE

¼ cup red wine vinegar

1 large garlic clove, grated

Kosher salt

½ cup extra-virgin olive oil

2 tablespoons smooth Dijon mustard

SOAK THE ONION: Fill a small bowl three-quarters full with cool water and some ice cubes. Sprinkle the onion slices into the water and submerge them. Refrigerate for at least 2 hours to soak out the raw onion flavor and make them juicier.

MAKE THE VINAIGRETTE: In a small bowl, whisk together the vinegar, garlic, mustard, and a few pinches of salt. Stream in the olive oil and 2 tablespoons cool water, whisking constantly. Taste for seasoning.

MAKE THE SALAD: Arrange the lettuce on a serving platter and sprinkle with the cucumber, tomatoes, and olives. Refrigerate for at least 1 hour, or up to 8 hours (cover if refrigerating more than an hour).

ASSEMBLE: Drain and dry the onion rounds. Spoon all of the dressing over the salad, sprinkle with the onions and oregano, and serve.

FENNEL, ORANGE
& CELERY ROOT SALAD

SERVES 4

When I was growing up, my dad brought home all kinds of cool vegetables from the supermarket, where he could spend 20 minutes in the produce section, picking out the perfect ingredients. (Don't get me started on how long it took him to pick out peaches or plums . . .) I asked him why he was so obsessed with produce and he said this: "I think I got my obsession with freshness from my grandmother. She would look at a tank filled with fresh, *live* lobsters and say to the fishmonger: 'They don't look fresh.'" Fennel was something he loved; celery root, too. The fennel had to feel tender and unblemished; the celery root had to feel heavy (therefore juicy and not dried out).

1 large bulb fennel

Zest and juice from 1 large lemon

3 tablespoons extra-virgin olive oil

Kosher salt

1 large navel orange, lightly zested, then peeled and flesh broken into sections, all juice reserved

1 large celery root, peeled and sliced into thin half-moons or diced

PREPARE THE FENNEL: Trim and discard the stalks and the tough outer layer from the fennel. Cut the bulb in half lengthwise and place the halves on a flat surface. Cut each half into thin slices, 12 to 14 per half. Arrange the fennel slices in a single layer (it's okay if some overlap) on a large serving platter.

MAKE THE DRESSING: In a large bowl, whisk the lemon juice and zest, 3 tablespoons of the olive oil, and a pinch of salt. Stir in the orange zest, sections, and juice, along with the celery root. Refrigerate for at least 1 hour, or up to 4 hours.

FINISH: Arrange the celery over the fennel, then spoon the dressing over top, coating each slice. Season with salt.

PS: Celery root has two layers of skin, so peel deeply.

CAPRESE SALAD

This beyond-classic salad traditionally intersperses tomato and mozzarella slices along with whole basil leaves in a circle on a platter. It is said to have originated on the island of Capri (hence: Caprese). I sometimes make it with small mozzarella balls (not too cold) and cherry tomatoes (must be chilled) to be more playful. I have also made this with breaded and fried mozzarella. You can get cute with some tarragon instead of basil, but honestly nothing beats basil, especially Genovese basil (if you see it, buy it).

DRESSING

¼ cup extra-virgin olive oil

3 tablespoons balsamic vinegar

2 tablespoons smooth Dijon mustard

SALAD

6 or 7 vine-ripened tomatoes, stemmed

1 pint cherry tomatoes, stemmed

Coarse sea salt and freshly ground black pepper

2 teaspoons sugar

2 (8-ounce) balls of fresh mozzarella cheese, each cut into 6 or 7 slices

Leaves from 4 sprigs fresh basil

MAKE THE DRESSING: In a large bowl, whisk together the olive oil and balsamic with the mustard and 1 tablespoon cool water. Taste for seasoning.

MAKE THE SALAD: On a flat surface, cut the vine-ripened tomatoes into slices and each cherry tomato in half. Arrange all of them in a single layer, flesh side up, on a large serving platter or individual plates. Season with coarse salt, black pepper, and the sugar.

ASSEMBLE: Intersperse the mozzarella slices with the tomatoes and drizzle with the dressing. Top with the basil leaves.

SERVE: This salad is not only delicious but also visually stunning. Let people see your hard work! Place the platter on the table and serve family style.

PS: Instead of fresh basil, try spooning pesto over the tomatoes and mozzarella.

CHOPPED SALAD
THAT COULD DOUBLE AS AN ITALIAN DELI SANDWICH

SERVES 4 TO 6

I get in deep with this chopped salad and enjoy the healthy aspect of it, the great textures, and the many variations. It's all about balance. Sometimes I'll let the cucumbers, radicchio, and carrots sit in the Dijon vinaigrette for a few minutes before tossing in the greens, so the mustard permeates the heartier vegetables. Most classic chopped salads have cubed or shredded cheeses and/or deli meats in the mix—to make this one vegetarian, leave out the meats and cut the provolone cheese into hearty cubes (rather than slicing) and then grate Parmesan cheese over the whole salad. The crispy chickpeas are tasty—if you want a shortcut, buy a bag at the store.

DRESSING

2 tablespoons smooth Dijon mustard

2 tablespoons fresh lemon juice

2 tablespoons red wine vinegar

⅔ cup extra-virgin olive oil

Kosher salt and freshly ground black pepper

CHICKPEAS

1 cup canola or avocado oil

1 cup cooked or low-sodium canned chickpeas, drained, rinsed, and dried (or skip the frying and use a bag of store-bought crispy chickpeas)

¼ teaspoon cayenne pepper

Kosher salt

SALAD

1 medium hothouse cucumber, peeled and cut into ½-inch dice

2 medium carrots, thinly sliced

2 medium heads of radicchio, cored and torn into bite-size pieces

2 cups arugula leaves

12 thin slices of provolone cheese, stacked and cut into thin strips

12 thin slices of spicy salami, stacked and cut into thin strips

6 thin slices of prosciutto, stacked and cut into thin strips

MAKE THE DRESSING: In a large bowl, whisk together the mustard, lemon juice, and vinegar. Whisk in the olive oil and 1 tablespoon cool water. Taste for seasoning.

FRY THE CHICKPEAS: In a medium pot, heat the canola oil over medium heat for about 3 minutes. Add a chickpea—if it's immediately surrounded by bubbles and sizzling, the oil is hot enough to fry. (If the chickpea isn't surrounded by bubbles, wait until it sizzles before adding the rest.) Line a baking sheet with a clean kitchen towel. Spoon the cayenne into a strainer. Thoroughly towel dry any moisture from the exterior of the chickpeas. When the oil is ready, use a slotted spoon to add the chickpeas carefully to the oil in batches and fry until crispy, 3 to 4 minutes. Again using the slotted spoon, transfer the chickpeas to the kitchen towel to drain. Season with salt and an even light "dusting" of the cayenne. Repeat with the remaining chickpeas, taking care to allow the oil to come back up to temperature between batches. If using store-bought fried chickpeas, skip this step.

ASSEMBLE THE SALAD: When ready to serve, toss the cucumber, carrots, radicchio, and arugula in the bowl with the dressing and stir to coat. Transfer the salad to a platter and sprinkle with the provolone, salami, and prosciutto. Sprinkle with the fried chickpeas and serve.

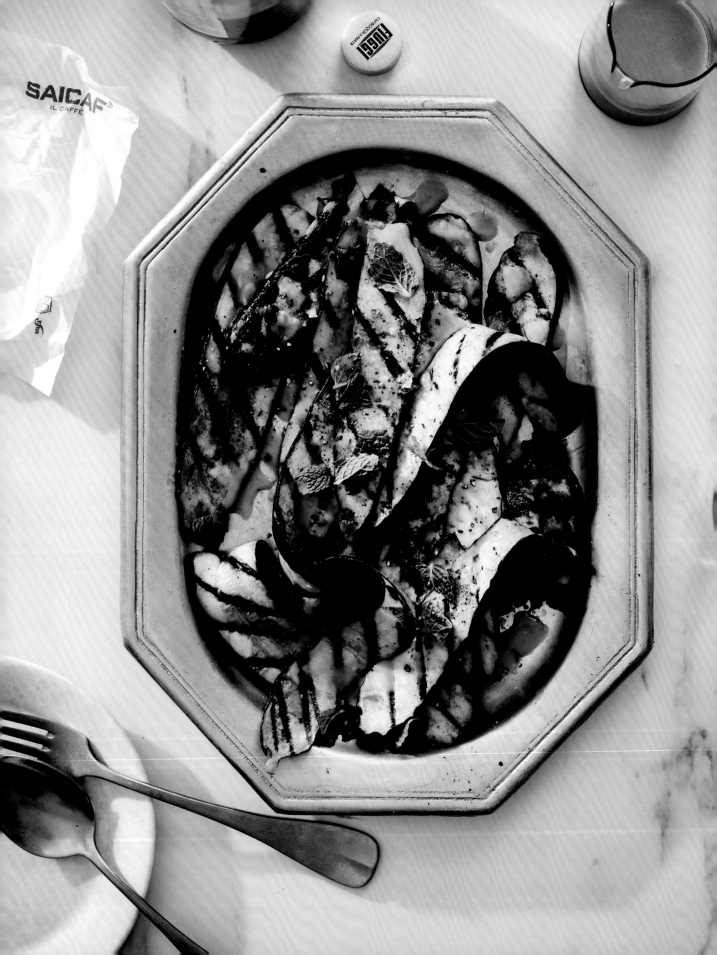

GRILLED ZUCCHINI & TOMATOES
WITH TORN MINT VINAIGRETTE

SERVES 4 TO 6

Fried zucchini dusted with Parmesan with a side of marinara sauce for dunking is, to my mind, the classic Italian American dish . . . so I decided to translate it into a salad! This is especially tasty paired with any tomato-based pasta dish or chicken cutlets. When grilling zucchini, if they are becoming overly charred but still aren't tender, scooch them over to a cooler part of the grill and finish cooking more slowly. Don't have a grill? Simply sear in a hot pan.

2 tablespoons red wine vinegar

2 tablespoons smooth Dijon mustard

2 tablespoons dark brown sugar

6 tablespoons extra-virgin olive oil

3 medium zucchini, cut lengthwise into ½-inch-thick slices

1 pint cherry tomatoes, stemmed and halved

¼ teaspoon cayenne pepper

Kosher salt

Leaves from 4 sprigs fresh mint

Maldon salt

MAKE THE DRESSING: In a large bowl, whisk together the vinegar, mustard, and 1 tablespoon of the brown sugar. Then, stream in 3 tablespoons of the olive oil and 1 tablespoon cool water, whisking constantly. Taste for seasoning.

Preheat the grill to medium-high heat.

SEASON THE ZUCCHINI: In a large bowl, combine the remaining 3 tablespoons of the olive oil, the zucchini slices, and cayenne. (For best results, "dust" the zucchini with the cayenne by putting it in a small strainer and sprinkling it evenly over the zucchini slices.) Toss to coat the zucchini with the oil. Season lightly with kosher salt.

GRILL THE ZUCCHINI: Arrange the zucchini in a single layer on one of the hottest parts of the grill and cook until they are tender to the touch and charred but not falling apart, 8 to 10 minutes total. (If the zucchini are larger, cook a few additional minutes, if needed.) Use a pair of metal tongs to remove the zucchini from the grill and arrange in a single layer directly on a large serving platter.

FINISH THE SALAD: Arrange the tomatoes, flesh side up, on top of the zucchini. Season with kosher salt and the remaining 1 tablespoon brown sugar. Tear up the mint leaves to help release their flavor and drizzle with about one-third of the dressing. Season with Maldon salt and serve with extra dressing on the side.

PS: There are lots of cool zucchini varietals available at farmers' markets, or as seeds if you have a green thumb. Romanesco, Gold Bar, and 8 Ball are a few of my favorites.

BURRATA
WITH FIGS

SERVES 4

Fresh figs, nectarines, peaches, or even plums would be nice here. Get what looks the ripest at your local market. The point is to get the sweetness of fruit and, ideally, the pleasant crunch of the fig seeds to go with this creamy cheese. You can also use dried figs. Figs transport me to either the beach in Italy or being a kid and tasting one my mom brought home from a specialty store. She would simply put the fruit out on a plate and the cheese on the side. She would sometimes use ricotta sprinkled with sugar. I love the extra richness burrata gives here. Don't be intimidated—burrata is just mozzarella's rich cousin that is finished with cream (instead of milk), making is looser and creamier.

1 pint fresh figs, halved (or 3 medium nectarines or peaches, pitted and quartered)

Juice from 1 large lemon

2 teaspoons sugar

2 cups arugula, coarsely chopped

2 tablespoons extra-virgin olive oil

1 to 2 balls burrata cheese (about 4 ounces each), dried of any excess moisture

Maldon salt

Freshly ground black pepper

SEASON THE FIGS AND ARUGULA: In a medium serving bowl, toss the figs with the lemon juice and sugar. Stir in the arugula and 1 tablespoon of the olive oil and toss gently.

FINISH: Gently center the burrata on top of the salad (use one or two balls depending on how decadent you're feeling) and sprinkle with salt and pepper.

SERVE: When serving, break the burrata with a spoon so everyone gets cheese with figs. Top with the remaining olive oil. Serve family style or spoon onto individual plates.

PS: If nectarines or apricots look riper than figs (or you can't find nice figs), use them instead. And don't mix fruits—for this salad, you want to taste the pure milk flavor of the burrata—and simplicity is the best way to get there.

STRACCIATELLA:
ITALIAN CHICKEN SOUP

SERVES 4 TO 6

This easy and hearty soup is based on a childhood favorite my mom made: stracciatella, which means "little rags" and references the eggs that are swirled into the soup to cook in the broth. My mother would make this but add lots of red pepper flakes (she loved spice in food) and didn't add spinach simply because my father didn't like it. The secret is not to overcook the chicken so you can shred the meat and return it to the broth. Acini di pepe, or "seeds of pepper," are a very small pasta that almost look like pearl couscous. If you can't find it, use any tiny macaroni shape.

2 tablespoons extra-virgin olive oil

3 medium carrots, cut into 1-inch rounds

3 medium celery stalks, cut into 1-inch pieces

24 pearl onions, peeled

Kosher salt and freshly ground black pepper

1 (3½- to 4-pound) whole chicken

6 cups chicken stock

6 sprigs fresh thyme

8 ounces acini di pepe pasta

3 large eggs, lightly beaten

2 cups baby spinach

½ cup finely grated Parmesan cheese

START THE SOUP: In a pot large enough to hold the chicken, add the olive oil, carrots, celery, and onions. Season the vegetables generously with salt and pepper and cook over medium heat, stirring, until the vegetables become translucent, 5 to 8 minutes. Add the chicken, stock, and thyme along with 3 cups water. Bring to a gentle simmer, skimming the surface with a ladle as impurities rise. Reduce the heat to low and cook slowly until the thickest part of a chicken thigh reaches an internal temperature of 165°F and the juices at the thigh joint run clear, 50 to 55 minutes.

COOK THE PASTA: Bring a medium pot of water to a boil and season with a generous handful of salt. It should taste like seawater. Drop the pasta in the water and cook until tender, 5 minutes. Drain the pasta in a fine-mesh strainer.

FINISH THE CHICKEN: Taste the chicken broth and adjust the seasoning. Use a slotted spoon and a pair of tongs to transfer the chicken to a large bowl. Let it cool for a few minutes and then remove and discard the skin. Remove the breast and thigh meat, taking care that there are no bones, and break the meat into bite-size pieces. Flake the meat off the wings.

FINISH THE SOUP: Remove and discard the thyme sprigs and heat the soup until piping hot. While stirring so the liquid is moving, gently stir in the eggs so they cook. Stir in the pasta. Season the chicken meat with salt and then stir it into the soup, along with the spinach and cheese, and serve.

PS: I've made this with my Thanksgiving turkey after almost all of the meat has been carved from the bones. It's deeply flavorful and comforting.

ITALIAN WEDDING SOUP

SERVES 4 TO 6

This recipe has many personal touches: The veal and chicken base I got from my mother; studding the chicken with a couple of cloves to add a special warm flavor I learned from making chicken stock at Guy Savoy in Paris; and most of all, the meatballs I inherited from my parents. It's a hybrid of a stock and a broth (flavor from cooking meat in the liquid), and while the techniques I call on are from my time working in French kitchens, the DNA of this soup is all about my mom's Italian cooking from Massachusetts.

BROTH

- 1 tablespoon extra-virgin olive oil
- 2 medium carrots, cut into 1½-inch rounds
- 2 medium celery stalks, cut into 1½-inch pieces
- 1 medium yellow onion, halved and thinly sliced
- Kosher salt and freshly ground black pepper
- 2 whole cloves
- 1 (3- to 4-pound) whole chicken
- 6 sprigs fresh thyme

MEATBALLS

- 8 ounces (½ pound) ground veal
- ½ cup panko breadcrumbs
- 3 tablespoons finely grated Parmesan cheese
- 2 large garlic cloves, minced
- Kosher salt
- 1 large egg, lightly beaten

TO FINISH

- 4 sprigs fresh basil, stemmed
- ½ cup finely grated Parmesan cheese
- 2 teaspoons red wine vinegar

MAKE THE BROTH: In a pot large enough to hold the chicken, warm the oil over medium heat. Add the carrots, celery, and onion and season generously with salt and pepper. Cook, stirring, until the vegetables become translucent, 3 to 5 minutes. Push the whole cloves into one of the chicken thighs and add it to the pot, along with the thyme and 6 cups water. Bring to a gentle simmer and skim the surface with a ladle as impurities rise. Sprinkle with a pinch of salt, then reduce the heat to low and cook slowly until the thickest part of a chicken thigh reaches an internal temperature of 165°F and the juices at the thigh joint run clear, 50 to 55 minutes.

MAKE THE MEATBALLS: Spread the veal across the bottom and sides of a medium bowl. Sprinkle with the breadcrumbs, Parmesan cheese, garlic, and 2 teaspoons salt. Add the egg and use your hands to blend the ingredients. Roll into meatballs about the size of small cherry tomatoes. (*Note*: Imperfectly rolled meatballs actually make this soup more homey and "real.") Arrange the meatballs in a single layer on a baking sheet and refrigerate for at least 1 hour.

FINISH THE CHICKEN: After about 45 minutes at a gentle simmer, taste the chicken broth and adjust the seasoning. Use a large spoon and a pair of tongs to transfer the chicken to a baking sheet or other flat surface and allow it to cool for a few minutes. Remove and discard the thyme sprigs. Take the breast and thigh meat off the chicken, taking care there are no bones, and break into bite-size pieces.

COOK THE MEATBALLS: Drop the meatballs into the soup and bring it back up to simmer. Allow it to simmer gently until the meatballs cook through, 12 to 15 minutes. Stir in the basil. Return the chicken meat to the soup and taste for seasoning. Sprinkle with Parmesan cheese and the vinegar and serve.

CLASSIC TOMATO MINESTRONE

SERVES 4 TO 6

While the backbone of minestrone is tomato, the perfect bite, to me at least, has a little pesto and some Parmesan cheese touched by the tomato and interrupted by the crunch of fresh vegetables. Then, bite two is when I dunk my crust of bread—preferably the Italian supermarket kind studded with sesame seeds that comes in the paper bag—and soak up all the liquid. *Note*: You can serve this recipe with basil pesto or make arugula pesto (page 145) for a little twist on a classic flavor.

¼ cup extra-virgin olive oil

24 to 30 pearl onions, peeled

2 large celery stalks, peeled and cut into ½-inch pieces

4 large garlic cloves, thinly sliced

¼ teaspoon red pepper flakes

Kosher salt

1 large Idaho potato, unpeeled, diced

1 (28-ounce) can peeled whole tomatoes with their juice

1 (15-ounce) can Great Northern or cannellini beans, drained and rinsed

½ bag frozen corn (5 to 6 ounces), thawed

½ cup finely grated Parmesan cheese

½ cup arugula pesto (page 145), for serving

Crusty bread, for serving

START THE SOUP: Heat a large, heavy-bottomed pot over medium heat. Add the olive oil, onions, celery, garlic, and red pepper flakes along with a generous pinch of salt. Cook, stirring with a wooden spoon, until the vegetables become tender, 5 to 8 minutes.

FINISH: Stir in the potato and cook until it starts to become tender, 2 to 3 minutes. Add the tomatoes and 2 cups water and continue cooking until the tomatoes start to break down, 15 to 18 minutes.

ASSEMBLE: Add the beans and corn. Simmer for 1 to 2 minutes, only to heat through. Remove from the heat and taste for seasoning. Stir in the Parmesan cheese and serve with pesto and bread on the side.

PS: If your soup is a little thin, a scoop of pesto stirred in just before serving thickens it.

SEAFOOD SALAD page 66

FISH & S

GRILLED OCTOPUS WITH WHITE BEANS page 72

CLAMS CASINO page 68

These are classic seafood dishes that remind me of those red-sauce-joint meals: sizzling clams, octopus with creamy white beans, and, of course, shrimp splashed with white wine and lemon. There is also a signature cioppino stew, linguine with clams (my mom's favorite), and steamed mussels with lots of garlic to round out the chapter.

LOBSTER FRA DIAVOLO page 80

HELL FISH

Dishes

SCALLOP GRATIN page 82

CALAMARI RIPIENI page 71

FEAST OF THE SEVEN FISHES

This is a very Italian American thing, with most families hosting a Feast of the Seven Fishes dinner on Christmas Eve. Traditionally, people ate fish because you weren't supposed to eat meat until Christmas Day, but as you can see from the menu here, there is nothing sacrificial about this spread!

While my parents were big on holiday traditions, we didn't do a special fish meal each year. Instead, we did it when the mood was right. (Whatever a snails mood might be.) The most successful meals like this are a mix of premade (precooked) elements with some cooking left to do last minute. It's similar to Thanksgiving in that way.

For the Feast of the Seven Fishes, I seek a balance of easy seafood elements and larger fish in the menu. I will make something to start, like an anchovy toast or Clams Casino, move into octopus, squid, or shrimp, and then into some larger fish. I like offering some canned sardines or smoked oysters for one course and then going bold with a fancy Shrimp Oreganata for the next. You can make the meal however you like as long as you strike a balance among the different genres of seafood and different textures. This is a meal to plan for and calculate its progression. I think a lot of the family bonding comes from the planning itself!

SEAFOOD SALAD • 66

CLAMS CASINO • 68

CALAMARI RIPIENI • 71

SHRIMP OREGANATA • 75

SCALLOP GRATIN • 82

SEARED SEA BASS
with Salmoriglio • 86

CIOPPINO • 90

SEEFOOD SALAD

SERVES 4 TO 6

This is a salad I have eaten so many times in NYC's Little Italy. Yes, it's labor intensive. And yes, the pay-off is amazing. Each bit of seafood should be fully cooked because the salad is chilled and served as is—this dish is not about reheating or keeping it warm. Taste as you go. Sample a mussel. Taste a clam. Get an idea of what it will taste like as a whole. The squid is seasoned with paprika and parsley to elevate it above the other seafood that have more personality, but really, it's the marinade of oregano, garlic, and lemon that soaks into the cooked seafoods and it's the slurping up of that broth/marinade ice cold that takes me to Mulberry Street. It's a refreshing first course or great for a springtime lunch. Serve with a loaf of bread to sop up the juices.

MARINADE

3 tablespoons extra-virgin olive oil

2 large garlic cloves, thinly sliced

Zest and juice from 1 large lemon

2 tablespoons smooth Dijon mustard

1 tablespoon capers plus 1 tablespoon of the brine

1 tablespoon red wine vinegar

2 teaspoons dried oregano

SEAFOOD

6 tablespoons extra-virgin olive oil

10 medium dry diver scallops, halved crosswise

Kosher salt and freshly ground black pepper

1 lemon, halved

(seafood continued)

3 pounds medium mussels, scrubbed under cold water

½ cup dry white wine

36 littleneck clams, scrubbed under cold water

2 pounds cleaned squid, tentacles and bodies separated, bodies cut into ½-inch-thick rounds

¼ teaspoon paprika

8 sprigs fresh flat-leaf parsley, finely chopped

3 large shallots, cut into thin rounds

3 medium celery stalks, peeled and cut into thin slices

4 sprigs fresh basil, stemmed (plus extra for serving; optional)

1 pint small cherry tomatoes, halved

1 large garlic clove

MAKE THE MARINADE: In a large serving bowl, whisk the olive oil with the garlic, lemon zest and juice, mustard, capers and their brine, vinegar, and oregano.

COOK THE SCALLOPS: Heat a large skillet over medium heat and add 2 tablespoons of the olive oil. Season the scallops on both sides with salt. When the oil begins to smoke lightly, use a pair of tongs to place each scallop, with space between them, in the hot oil. Cook until they brown on the first side, 2 minutes. Lift them up off the pan and place them back down again without turning them to their second sides and cook for 1 minute more. Moving them repositions them freshly in the hot pan and encourages further browning. It also ensures they are not sticking. Turn the scallops onto their second sides and cook for an additional 2 minutes, until lightly browned and cooked through. Lift them up off the pan and place them back down again, without turning, and cook for 1 minute more. Remove the scallops from the pan and place on a platter. Squeeze the juice from one lemon half over them and transfer to the bowl with the marinade.

COOK THE MUSSELS: Rinse the mussels one final time to make sure they are free of any sand or grit. In the same large skillet, add 1 tablespoon of the olive oil and then the mussels in as close to a single layer as you can. Return the pan to high heat, add ¼ cup of the white wine, and cook, shaking the pan slightly, until all of the mussels open, 3 to 5 minutes (if any don't open after 5 minutes, discard them). Turn off the heat. When the mussels have cooled for about 5 minutes, transfer to a large bowl, shell them, and add the meat to the bowl with the scallops. Strain any cooking liquid through a fine-mesh sieve over the bowl with the scallops.

COOK THE CLAMS: Rinse the clams one final time to make sure they are free of any sand or grit. Using the same skillet, add 1 tablespoon of the olive oil and then the clams in as close to a single layer as you can. Return the pan to high heat, add the remaining ¼ cup white wine, and cook, shaking the pan slightly, until all of the clams open and the liquid evaporates, 3 to 5 minutes (if any don't open after 5 minutes, discard them). Turn off the heat. When the clams have cooled for about 5 minutes, transfer to a large bowl, shell, and add the meat to the scallops and mussels. Strain any cooking liquid through a fine-mesh sieve into the bowl with the scallops and mussels.

COOK THE SQUID: Return the large skillet to high heat and add 1 tablespoon of the olive oil. When the oil begins to smoke lightly, remove the pan from the heat, add the squid, return the pan to the heat, and cook until the squid is no longer translucent, 2 to 3 minutes. Dust with the paprika and sprinkle with the parsley. Remove the squid from the pan and squeeze the juice from the remaining lemon half over them. Add all to the other seafood.

COOK THE SHALLOTS AND CELERY: Return the large skillet to medium heat and add the remaining 1 tablespoon olive oil, the shallots, and celery. Season with salt and pepper. Cook, stirring, until the vegetables are translucent, 3 to 5 minutes. Add the vegetables to the seafood mix. Stir in the basil, cherry tomatoes, and garlic. Refrigerate until fully chilled, at least 2 hours, or up to 8 hours.

SERVE: When ready to serve, spoon the salad into individual bowls and spoon any marinade from the bowl over the top. Finish with a little basil if you like.

CLAMS CASINO

SERVES 4 TO 6

For this dish, my mother took inspiration from her New England upbringing and the red-sauce joints we'd visit on Mulberry Street in Little Italy. She made me realize that Clams Casino is great to make at home—it's so easy to assemble and there are never any leftovers . . . it's also the perfect party dish since the clams can be prepped out completely, then frozen and baked straight from the freezer. If you bake from frozen, just allow the frozen ones to cook a few minutes more to make sure they are bubbling and hot in the center. You can also assemble, refrigerate, and bake them off last minute. Small note about the bacon: I don't like when bacon is undercooked, so I precook it a little and let the broiler finish the work.

36 littleneck clams, scrubbed under cold water

5 tablespoons unsalted butter, at room temperature

2 tablespoons dry vermouth

9 thin strips bacon, each cut into 4 pieces

2 whole scallions, minced

4 large garlic cloves, minced

Zest and juice from 1 large lemon, plus (optional) lemon wedges for serving

Kosher salt and freshly ground black pepper

⅔ cup panko breadcrumbs

12 sprigs flat-leaf parsley, coarsely chopped, stems and all

¾ cup heavy cream

1 tablespoon Worcestershire sauce

1 teaspoon Tabasco sauce

COOK THE CLAMS: Heat a large skillet over high heat. Rinse the clams one final time to make sure they are free of any grit. Add 1 tablespoon of the butter to the skillet, add the clams and vermouth, and cook, shaking the pan slightly, until the clams open, 3 to 5 minutes. Transfer each clam as it opens to a large bowl (if any don't open after 5 minutes, discard them).

COOK THE BACON: Arrange the bacon pieces in the bottom of a large skillet and add 2 tablespoons of water. Cook over medium heat just until the water evaporates and the bacon starts to cook through without browning (it won't be crisp or fully cooked). Remove the bacon to a plate and set aside. Save the bacon grease.

Preheat the oven to 350°F.

MAKE THE BREADCRUMB MIX: In a medium bowl, combine the scallions, garlic, and lemon zest and juice. Season with salt and pepper and mix in the breadcrumbs, remaining 4 tablespoons butter, 2 tablespoons of the reserved bacon grease, and the parsley.

PREPARE AND BAKE THE CLAMS: Twist off the top shell from each clam. This leaves the clam "meat" in its bottom shell. Slide a small knife under the clam meat to loosen it, but leave it in the original spot in its shell. In a small bowl, combine the cream, Worcestershire, and Tabasco. Spoon a touch of the cream mixture on top of each clam and immediately mold some of the breadcrumb mixture into each so the clam body is covered. Arrange them in a single layer on a baking sheet. Put a piece of bacon on top of each.

COOK THE CLAMS: Bake until heated through, 10 to 12 minutes. Preheat the broiler and broil the clams for 1 to 2 minutes, until bubbly and browned, watching them constantly so the bacon doesn't burn.

SERVE: Arrange 6 to 8 clams on individual serving plates. Serve with additional lemon wedges on the side, if desired.

PS: You can also make and broil mussels in the same way.

CALAMARI RIPIENI

SERVES 4 TO 6

I think one of the great things about being Italian American is that you can tack on one Italian word to a classic dish and dinner just sounds like it's going to be even more delicious. "Ripieni" refers to musical instruments working together in a piece, while "ripieno" means stuffed—and this dish exemplifies both ideas. Get squid at the fish counter (look for medium squid—they're more tender than larger ones) and clean it yourself (see the tip, below), or buy frozen and simply defrost.

- 3 tablespoons extra-virgin olive oil
- 2 medium yellow onions, halved and thinly sliced
- 5 yellow inner stalks of celery, cut into thin slices
- 1 large red bell pepper, cored, seeded, and diced
- 2 large garlic cloves, minced
- ½ teaspoon red pepper flakes
- Kosher salt and freshly ground black pepper
- 12 medium squid (about 2 pounds total), cleaned, tentacles finely chopped, bodies cleaned and kept whole
- ½ cup panko breadcrumbs
- ¼ cup cooked Great Northern or cannellini beans
- Juice of 1 large lemon
- 10 sprigs fresh flat-leaf parsley, stemmed

MAKE THE STUFFING: In a large skillet set over medium heat, heat 1 tablespoon of the olive oil. When the oil begins to smoke lightly, add the onions, celery, bell pepper, garlic, and red pepper flakes. Season with salt and stir to blend. Cook, stirring, until translucent, 3 to 5 minutes. Stir in the chopped tentacles and cook for 2 minutes more, until cooked through and no longer opaque. Set aside to cool.

STUFF THE SQUID: Arrange the squid bodies on a baking sheet and season with salt and pepper. Use a small spoon to fill the squid bodies with an even amount of the stuffing, then close each opening with a toothpick. There's no need to overfill—just fill so you get enough stuffing as you cut and eat the squid. Refrigerate for at least 1 hour and up to 8 hours.

COOK THE SQUID: Heat a medium sauté pan over medium heat. Add the remaining 2 tablespoons olive oil. When it begins to smoke lightly, remove the pan from the heat and add the squid. Return the pan to the heat and cook quickly, using a pair of tongs to rotate them after each minute, until the squid are no longer translucent, 4 to 6 minutes. Drain any excess oil and transfer the squid to a baking sheet. Stir the breadcrumbs into the pan to absorb the juices, then spoon the breadcrumbs over the squid.

FINISH: In the same pan set over medium heat, combine the beans with a splash of water and simmer, mashing them with the back of a spoon, until the liquid thickens with the starch from the beans. Add the lemon juice. Spoon the beans and lemon over the squid or spoon the beans onto individual plates and top with the squid and parsley (or serve the beans on the side).

PS: If you buy the squid fresh and want to clean it yourself, first separate the tentacles from the body. Next, remove the outer layer of purplish skin and the clear (almost plastic-looking) cartilage from inside the body. If sandy, rinse and pat dry. Trim and discard the eyes from the tentacles. Refrigerate until ready to cook.

GRILLED OCTOPUS
WITH WHITE BEANS

SERVES 4 TO 6

This is exactly the kind of dish you can get at a fancy red-sauce joint that brings such a strong contrast to the classic tomato sauce–laden dishes that are on the table. It introduces lightness, citrus, and spice, plus char from the grill to contrast the acidity and sweetness of the orange. If you don't have a grill or grill pan, simply sear the octopus in a hot skillet instead.

2 precooked octopuses (1½ to 2 pounds each, preferably just tentacles)

2 tablespoons extra-virgin olive oil

1 large garlic clove, grated

Zest and juice from 1 large lemon, plus (optional) lemon wedges for serving

Kosher salt

1 medium navel orange, peeled, broken into sections

1 cup cooked Great Northern beans

¼ small Fresno chile, cut into thin rounds and seeded

Preheat the grill to medium-high heat.

GET READY: Cut the tentacles from each octopus and discard the heads. Toss the tentacles with 1 tablespoon of the olive oil. In a medium bowl, combine the remaining 1 tablespoon olive oil, the garlic, lemon zest and juice, and a pinch of salt.

GRILL THE OCTOPUS: Place the octopus tentacles in a single layer on the hot grill and cook until they char, 2 to 3 minutes. Continue to cook on all sides, rotating every 2 to 3 minutes, for a total of 12 to 15 minutes. The octopus should feel tender to the touch but not yielding or falling apart. Remove from the grill.

FINISH: Toss the octopus in the bowl with the olive oil mixture. Gently mix in the orange sections, white beans, and chile slices. Taste for seasoning and serve.

SHRIMP OREGANATA

SERVES 4

This dish feels like a throwback to my mom or grandmother's simpler style of cooking, where the shrimp are oven baked and then run under the broiler last minute. The flavor is different than when you bake seafood: To me, baking it brings out those naturally briny and sweet flavors. I also like that the shrimp are really cooked through and piping hot. Hot food is underrated! To that end, it feels like these shrimp could easily be cooking alongside some pizzas or gratin dishes of baked ziti at a red-sauce joint. Get everything together and then heat and serve when ready.

1½ pounds colossal (10-count) shrimp (about 16 shrimp), shelled and deveined

5 tablespoons extra-virgin olive oil

Kosher salt

¼ teaspoon red pepper flakes

⅔ cup panko breadcrumbs

8 sprigs fresh flat-leaf parsley, coarsely chopped, stems and all

2 tablespoons finely grated pecorino cheese

2 teaspoons dried oregano

1 large lemon, zested and halved, plus (optional) additional lemon wedges for serving

½ cup dry white wine

1 teaspoon Worcestershire sauce

Fresh oregano leaves, optional

Preheat the oven to 450°F. Position a rack in the center of the oven.

GET READY: In a large bowl, toss the shrimp with 2 tablespoons of the olive oil to coat. Arrange, with space between each, in a single layer on a baking sheet. Season with salt and sprinkle with the red pepper flakes.

MAKE THE BREADCRUMB MIX: In another medium bowl, combine the remaining 3 tablespoons olive oil, the breadcrumbs, parsley, pecorino, oregano, and lemon zest.

BAKE THE SHRIMP: Pour the white wine and Worcestershire in the bottom of the baking sheet. Spoon the breadcrumb mix over each shrimp. Bake on the center rack until the shrimp turn pink and are no longer translucent, 8 to 10 minutes.

FINISH: Preheat the broiler. Run the shrimp under the broiler until golden brown and bubbling, 1 to 2 minutes. Squeeze the lemon juice over the tops. Serve right away with additional lemon wedges and fresh oregano sprinkled on top, if desired.

SHRIMP RISOTTO
WITH CHERRY TOMATOES

SERVES 4 TO 6

This dish is a story of naturally sweet mascarpone and Arborio rice meeting up with briny shrimp and tart cherry tomatoes. The cardinal rule in Italian cooking—no cheese with fish—is broken here by both the mascarpone and the Parmesan, but they give so much umami flavor and natural salty and creamy notes that the potential wrist slap is worth it. Don't be afraid of risotto. Just add the liquid in increments so that when the rice is cooked there isn't a ton of liquid left in the pan. Perfect risotto should have some looseness, with the liquid being naturally starchy from the rice.

4 tablespoons extra-virgin olive oil

1¼ cups Arborio rice

Maldon salt

2 medium shallots, minced

⅓ cup dry white wine

½ cup (4 ounces) mascarpone cheese

¾ cup finely grated Parmesan cheese

1½ pounds colossal (10-count) shrimp (about 16 shrimp), peeled, deveined, and cut into thirds

Kosher salt and freshly ground black pepper

1 large garlic clove, minced

1 pint small cherry tomatoes, halved (or left whole)

1 large lemon, halved

Fresh oregano, for serving (optional)

TOAST THE RICE: Heat about 1 quart water in a medium pot until simmering. In a large sauté pan over medium heat, combine 2 tablespoons of the olive oil and the rice and season with salt. Using a wooden spoon, stir to coat the rice with the oil and then smooth it gently so it's in a uniform layer in the pan. When you hear the sound of the rice popping and smell the rice getting nutty, 2 to 3 minutes, stir the rice, then cook undisturbed so another layer toasts gently, 1 to 2 minutes.

COOK THE RICE: Stir in the shallots with a pinch of salt and reduce the heat to medium-low. Cook, stirring with a wooden spoon, until the shallots are translucent, 2 to 3 minutes. Add the white wine and cook, stirring constantly, until the wine evaporates. Ladle enough of the hot water into the pan to just cover the rice. Simmer, uncovered and stirring constantly, until the rice has absorbed a fair amount of the liquid.

FINISH THE RICE: From this point, it should take 15 to 18 minutes to finish the risotto. Add the water in small increments, keeping the rice lightly covered and simmering, and cook, stirring frequently, until the rice is tender but still has a firm bite, like pasta cooked al dente, 15 to 18 minutes. Turn off the heat and stir in the mascarpone and Parmesan cheese into the rice. Let it sit on the stove with the heat off while you sear the shrimp.

SEAR THE SHRIMP: Season the shrimp on both sides with kosher salt and pepper. Heat a large skillet set over high heat and add the remaining 2 tablespoons oil. When the oil begins to smoke lightly, add the shrimp in a single layer and cook until lightly browned, 2 to 3 minutes. Shake the pan gently to move the shrimp around as they finish cooking. Cook the shrimp for an additional 2 to 3 minutes, until they are no longer translucent. Stir in the garlic and cherry tomatoes and squeeze the lemon juice over them.

SERVE: Spoon the risotto into individual bowls and top with the shrimp, tomatoes, and pan juices over each (or transfer the risotto to a serving bowl, top with everything, and serve family style). Serve sprinkled with oregano if you like.

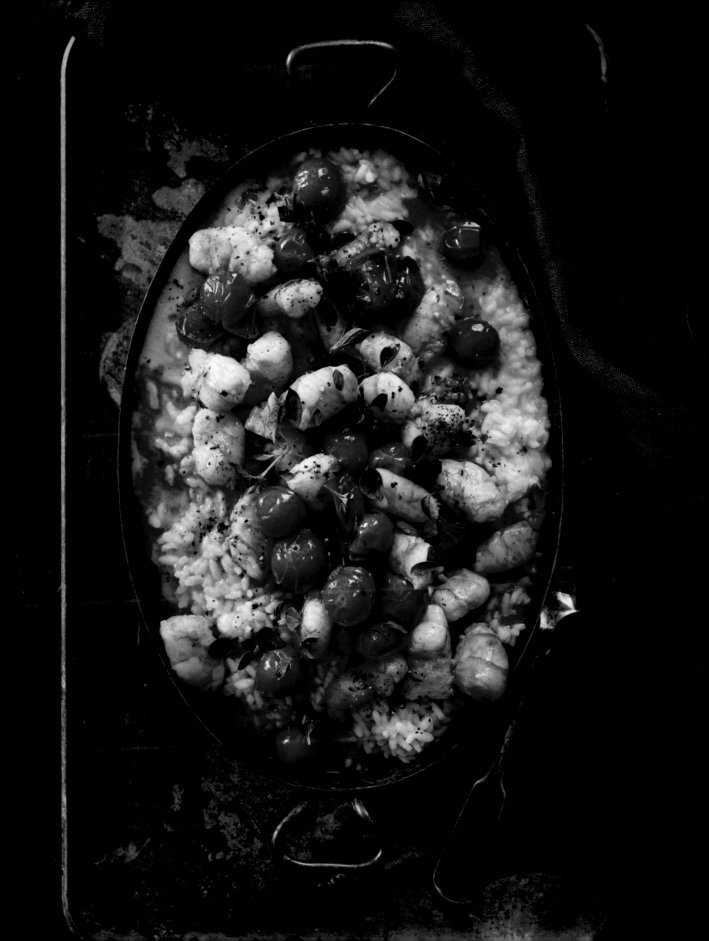

MUSSELS
WITH CINZANO & GARLIC

SERVES 4

Why Cinzano? After all, won't white wine or the dry vermouth I use to make a martini do? While I am not often one who insists on a specific wine for anything and believe that the "cheap stuff" is perfectly fine since most of the tastes cook out, these mussels are an exception. Cinzano, a sweet vermouth infused with cinnamon, clove, and citrus, brings acidity and nuance to the mussels that simultaneously evokes their natural sweetness. Plus, it's not pricey and makes a great spritzer to go with the mussels (just add sparkling water and a generous squeeze of fresh lemon). A little squeeze of lemon for the mussels also complements the floral notes from the Cinzano. For a fun companion, serve with bowls of salt and vinegar potato chips. Did I mention this comes together in roughly 20 minutes?

4 pounds fresh small to medium mussels, thoroughly rinsed and debearded

4 tablespoons (½ stick) unsalted butter

1 cup Cinzano vermouth

8 large garlic cloves, thinly sliced

Juice from 1 lemon

Kosher salt (if needed for seasoning)

COOK THE MUSSELS: Heat a large skillet over high heat. Rinse the mussels one final time to make sure they are free of any sand or grit. Remove the pan from the heat and add 2 tablespoons of the butter to the hot skillet, then add the mussels in as close to a single layer as you can. Return the pan to the heat, add the Cinzano, and cook, shaking the pan slightly, until all of the mussels open, 3 to 5 minutes. Remove the mussels and transfer to a large bowl (if any don't open after 5 minutes, discard them). Add the garlic to the skillet and reduce the heat to medium-low. Simmer the liquid until the garlic softens and there is no raw alcohol flavor, 3 to 5 minutes.

FINISH: Remove the skillet from the heat and stir in the remaining 2 tablespoons butter. Return the mussels to the pan and warm over medium heat while basting with a large spoon to coat with the sauce. Squirt the lemon juice over the top and taste for seasoning.

SERVE: Transfer the mussels and sauce to a large bowl or serve them directly from the skillet. Place the mussels in the center of the table with bowls for each serving and additional bowls for the empty shells.

LOBSTER FRA DIAVOLO

SERVES 4

"Fra Diavolo" loosely means "Brother Devil" (or "among the Devil"), referring to an Italian bandit and the pepper flakes and hot sauce that give this dish its signature heat! You can use lobster tails or cut-up whole lobsters (or frankly, simply replace the lobster with shrimp, mussels, or clams). You can also remove the lobster meat from the shells when cooked through and serve the meat and sauce over bowls of angel hair pasta. If you buy cooked lobster tails, simply skip the first two steps and add the meat at the end, when the sauce is fully made, and warm the lobster through. I use sambal hot sauce—which is Indonesian, not Italian—because I like its roughish texture and heat, but Calabrian chiles are also excellent here and the more traditional choice. You can easily adjust the spice level by reducing the amount of hot sauce and omitting the red pepper flakes. Serve with pasta on the side or hot garlic bread.

4 (½-pound/8-ounce) lobster tails

¼ cup extra-virgin olive oil

1 tablespoon tomato paste

1 medium carrot, cut into thin rounds

1 medium yellow onion, minced

2 large garlic cloves, minced

½ teaspoon red pepper flakes

Kosher salt

¼ cup brandy

½ cup dry white wine

1 pint cherry tomatoes, halved

2 tablespoons unsalted butter

1 tablespoon low-sodium soy sauce

1 tablespoon sambal oelek chile paste

1 tablespoon red wine vinegar

1 small bunch fresh chives, cut into 1-inch pieces

PREP THE LOBSTER TAILS: Using a sharp knife on a flat surface, cut each tail in half lengthwise.

SEAR THE TAILS: Heat the olive oil in a large sauté pan over medium heat. When the oil begins to smoke lightly, remove the pan from the heat and add the lobster tail halves, flesh side down. Return the pan to medium-low heat and cook for 2 to 3 minutes, just to brown the meat slightly without cooking it through. Remove the tails from the pan.

BUILD THE SAUCE: Add the tomato paste to the same pan and raise the heat to medium. Gently fry the paste so it cooks in the oil and develops great flavor, 2 to 3 minutes. Add the carrot, onion, and garlic and season with the red pepper flakes and a generous pinch of salt. Cook, stirring, until the onion becomes translucent, 3 to 5 minutes. Add the brandy and cook until almost all of the liquid is gone, 2 to 3 minutes. Don't rush this step or you will have a raw alcohol taste in your sauce.

FINISH THE SAUCE: When the brandy has evaporated, add the white wine and cook until almost all of the liquid is gone. Add ½ cup water and the tomatoes and simmer until the sauce comes together, 3 to 5 minutes, stirring occasionally. Whisk in the butter, soy sauce, and chile paste. Taste for seasoning.

ASSEMBLE: Carefully return the lobster tails to the sauce. Cook gently over medium heat, basting the lobster with the sauce, until the lobster meat is fully cooked, 3 to 5 minutes. Stir in the vinegar and sprinkle with the chives. Serve family style from the skillet or on individual plates.

SCALLOP GRATIN

SERVES 4

One bite of this simple seafood dish (made sac-rilegiously with cheese!) takes me straight back to my first memories of the broiling-hot clams at Umbertos or the steaming (boiling!) hot mussels at Il Cortile—both on Mulberry Street in Little Italy. My mother made these cheesy scallops right in the actual scallop shells. I find that seafood served in shells creates the drama and sizzle at the table that awakens the inner appetite and makes food exhilarating and theatrical, yet also true to its natural form at the same time. The layering of the ingredients in the sauce is important—you need to let the wine cook out to avoid a raw alcohol fla-vor, and the sauce has to cool slightly so the cream and lemon juice don't link up and curdle.

¾ cup panko breadcrumbs

2 tablespoons unsalted butter, at room temperature

¾ cup finely shredded Gruyère cheese

½ cup finely grated Parmesan cheese

6 sprigs fresh thyme, stemmed

Kosher salt and freshly ground black pepper

2 tablespoons extra-virgin olive oil

16 medium dry diver sea scallops (in their shells, if possible; shells reserved), each cut in half horizontally

2 medium shallots, minced

2 large garlic cloves, minced

½ pound (8 ounces) small white button mushrooms, thinly sliced

¼ cup dry vermouth

1 cup heavy cream

3 scallions, green and white parts, thinly sliced

Juice from 1 large lemon, plus (optional) additional lemon wedges for serving

MAKE THE TOPPING: In a mixing bowl, use a rubber spatula to combine the breadcrumbs and butter. Mix in the Gruyère and Parmesan cheeses and the thyme. Season with salt and pepper.

COOK THE SCALLOPS: Heat a large skillet over medium-high heat and add 1 tablespoon of the olive oil. When the oil begins to smoke lightly, season the scallops with salt and pepper and add half to the pan, with space between each. Cook for 2 minutes to brown slightly on one side and use a metal spatula to quickly remove them. Repeat with the remaining 1 tablespoon of olive oil and scallops. Set the scallops aside.

MAKE THE SAUCE: Add the shallots and garlic to the same pan, season with salt and pepper, and reduce the heat to medium. Cook, stirring, until translucent, 2 to 3 minutes. Add the mushrooms and cook for 2 to 3 minutes more, until browned and no longer "weeping" water. Remove the pan from the heat and carefully add the vermouth. Return the pan to the heat and cook until all of the liquid has evaporated. Add the cream, reduce the heat to low, and simmer, stirring gently, until the mixture thickens, 5 to 7 minutes. (*Note:* Do not let the mixture boil vigorously or it risks separating.) Remove the pan from the heat and allow to cool slightly, 10 to 15 minutes.

ASSEMBLE: Preheat the broiler. Stir the scallops, scallions, and lemon juice into the cream mixture. Transfer the sauce and scallops to a shallow ovenproof dish, arranging in a single layer (or, if you have the scallop shells, make individual servings with two scallop rounds per shell).

BROIL THE SCALLOPS: Sprinkle the breadcrumbs over the scallops and broil until bubbling and browned, 2 to 3 minutes. (*Note:* The time may be slightly longer or shorter depending on how quickly the tops brown. Watch carefully!)

SERVE: Arrange the scallops on individual plates and serve with additional lemon wedges, if desired.

**SEARED SEA BASS
WITH SALMORIGLIO** page 86

SEARED SEA BASS
WITH SALMORIGLIO

SERVES 4

The word "salmoriglio" is Sicilian—it means "a light brine." And truly, it has such a nice ring to it (it's the kind of last name I wish I grew up with). It is seen as more of a condiment than a sauce in Sicily and, since my mother's family is from Calabria, I make this recipe in honor of her. Made with parsley, oregano, lemon, and garlic, it can be smeared on seafood or meats, but I particularly love it with something clean and flaky, like bass, cod, and flounder. It would be smart to make a double batch of the sauce and store it in your fridge for up to 2 weeks (although it likely won't ever hang around that long). Spread it on your weeknight chicken or a weekend steak. I even put it on cauliflower steaks for meatless Monday.

5 tablespoons extra-virgin olive oil

Kosher salt

12 to 14 sprigs fresh flat-leaf parsley (stems and all), coarsely chopped

Leaves from 3 to 4 sprigs fresh oregano

Juice from 2 large lemons

2 large garlic cloves, minced

1 teaspoon dried oregano

1 teaspoon garlic powder

4 (6-ounce) skin-on striped sea bass fillets, bones removed

Preheat the oven to 350°F.

MAKE THE SAUCE: In a medium bowl, whisk together 3 tablespoons of the olive oil with 2 tablespoons cool water and a pinch of salt. Vigorously whisk in the parsley, fresh oregano, lemon juice, garlic, dried oregano, and garlic powder. Taste for seasoning.

COOK THE FISH: Heat a large skillet over high heat and add the remaining 2 tablespoons oil. When the oil begins to smoke lightly, remove the pan from the heat and one by one add the bass fillets, skin side down and leaving space between each. Return the pan to the heat and cook until the skin becomes crispy, 5 to 8 minutes. The flesh should be moving from opaque to white. Use a metal spatula to turn the fish and cook until the fish is cooked through, 3 to 5 minutes. (To check doneness, touch the fish in the center—it should feel firm but still slightly yielding.) Transfer the fish to plates or a platter and spoon the sauce over or serve on the side.

SWORDFISH PICCATA

SERVES 4

Piccata sauce, made with shallots, lemon, capers, and white wine, is classically Italian, though it could easily pass as French. It's a really close cousin of Francese sauce, which has a similar combination, usually with no capers (see Chicken Francese, page 153). I use curly parsley here to stand up to the salty and acidic sauce: It's grassy and a welcome surprise. In addition to swordfish, this sauce works well with tuna steaks off the grill or bass or cod, too. You could also toss the sauce with roasted clams, mussels, or shrimp.

2 tablespoons extra-virgin olive oil

4 (6-ounce) swordfish steaks

Kosher salt and freshly ground black pepper

2 tablespoons unsalted butter, cubed

3 large shallots, cut into ¼-inch-thick rounds

2 dried bay leaves

1 cup dry white wine

10 to 12 sprigs fresh curly parsley (stems and all), coarsely chopped

1 tablespoon capers, plus a splash of their brine

Zest and juice from 1 lemon

Maldon salt

COOK THE FISH: Heat a large sauté pan over high heat and add the oil. Season the swordfish on both sides with kosher salt and pepper. When the oil begins to smoke lightly, remove the pan from the heat and, one by one, add the fish to the pan, leaving space between each. Return the pan to the heat and cook until the first sides brown, 3 to 5 minutes. Using a metal spatula, turn each piece of fish and cook until the swordfish is cooked through, not pink or cold in the middle, another 3 to 5 minutes. Remove the fish from the pan and transfer to a baking sheet to rest while you make the sauce.

MAKE THE SAUCE: In the same pan where you cooked the fish, melt 1 tablespoon of the butter. Add the shallots and bay leaves and reduce the heat to medium-low. Cook, stirring, until translucent and tender, 5 to 8 minutes. Add the white wine and reduce until there is only about 2 tablespoons of wine remaining, 3 to 5 minutes. Slowly whisk in the remaining 1 tablespoon butter in small increments. Season with kosher salt and pepper. Keep warm.

FINISH: Remove the bay leaves from the sauce and add the parsley and capers and a splash of their brine. Spoon the sauce over the fish a few times to glaze it. Squeeze lemon juice over the fish, add the zest, and sprinkle with Maldon salt before serving. Serve the fish directly from the pan or transfer the fish and sauce to a serving platter.

LINGUINE ALLA VONGOLE

This is not a dish for fresh pasta—it actually begs for the "tooth" of hearty, chewy pasta. The "vongole," or clams, are pleasantly chewy, too. It's classic with linguine, but I like a thicker pasta for this, maybe bucatini, though Mom would use perciatelli. The clams and their briny liquid contrasting with the pasta with its hint of butter, garlic, and herbs are so simple and yet so pleasing.

1 cup dry white wine

8 ounces bottled clam juice

1 dried bay leaf

3 dozen littleneck clams, thoroughly rinsed

2 tablespoons extra-virgin olive oil

4 large garlic cloves, minced

Kosher salt

10 to 12 ounces canned baby or chopped clams, such as Bar Harbor or Cento brand

2 tablespoons unsalted butter

1 pound bucatini or perciatelli pasta

12 sprigs fresh flat-leaf parsley, coarsely chopped, stems and all

Juice from 1 lemon

COOK THE CLAMS: Heat a large skillet over medium heat. Add 1 cup water and the white wine, clam juice, and bay leaf. Bring to a simmer and reduce the liquid by about half. Rinse the clams one final time to make sure they are free of any sand or grit. Add the clams in a single layer and cook until they open, 5 to 8 minutes. Use a pair of metal tongs to transfer the clams as they open to a large bowl (if any don't open after 8 minutes, discard them). Strain the cooking liquid through a double layer of cheesecloth or a coffee filter to remove sand and reserve the liquid separately. Shell the clams.

MAKE THE SAUCE: Wipe out the pan and set it over low heat. Add the olive oil and garlic, season with salt, and cook, stirring occasionally, until the garlic becomes translucent, 3 to 5 minutes. Add the canned and fresh clams and their strained cooking liquid and simmer over low heat for 1 minute. Whisk in the butter and taste for seasoning.

COOK THE PASTA: Meanwhile, in a large pot, bring 6 quarts water to a rolling boil. Add 2 tablespoons salt; the pasta water should taste like seawater. Add the pasta and stir from time to time as it cooks so it doesn't stick to the bottom. Cook the pasta until al dente, chewy but not hard or raw tasting, 8 to 10 minutes. Drain the pasta in a colander.

FINISH: Add the pasta to the pan with the clams and sauce. Remove and discard the bay leaf. Add the parsley and lemon juice and toss to blend. Taste for seasoning and serve.

CIOPPINO

●

SERVES 4 TO 6

Both cioppino and bouillabaisse are flavorful fish soups that could almost be called a light stew. French bouillabaisse is all about how the fish flavors and thickens the broth as it simmers and the fish falls apart. Italian cioppino differs in that, generally, it uses more textured and briny fish and shellfish that really stand up to acidic tomato and floral saffron. Homemade aioli, traditionally made with egg yolks and olive oil, is delicious, but I love a shortcut, so I just make mine with mayonnaise. This soup is for slurping and soaking up with slices of bread. You could even put it in a bread bowl . . . then all you have to do is close your eyes and imagine yourself by the ocean in Italy . . . or at a great red-sauce joint in Jersey.

SOUP

- 5 tablespoons extra-virgin olive oil
- 2 pounds cod, hake, or pollock fillets, cut into 1-inch-thick slices
- Kosher salt
- 2 pounds mussels, scrubbed
- 2 cups dry white wine
- 24 littleneck clams, scrubbed
- 3 bunches of scallions (green and white parts), minced
- 4 garlic cloves, minced
- 6 sprigs fresh thyme, tied together with string
- ½ teaspoon saffron threads, lightly chopped
- 1 (28-ounce) can peeled whole tomatoes
- 2 cups store-bought fish stock or 8 ounces bottled clam juice plus 8 ounces water

AIOLI

- 4 tablespoons mayonnaise
- 3 large garlic cloves, grated
- 1 tablespoon Worcestershire sauce
- ½ teaspoon Tabasco
- Kosher salt
- 2 limes
- Sourdough bread, toasted, for serving

COOK THE FISH: Heat a large skillet over high heat and add 2 tablespoons of the olive oil. Season the fish pieces with salt. When the oil begins to smoke, add the fish in a single layer and cook until browned, 3 to 4 minutes. Use metal tongs to turn the fish and cook for an additional 2 to 3 minutes, until cooked through and no longer opaque. Transfer the fish to a baking sheet and set aside.

COOK THE MUSSELS AND CLAMS: In the same skillet over medium heat, combine the mussels and 1 cup of the white wine. Simmer the mussels for 3 to 5 minutes, transferring each to a large bowl as it opens (if any don't open after 5 minutes, discard them). When all of the mussels have been cooked, add the clams to the pan and the remaining 1 cup white wine. Cook the clams for 5 to 8 minutes, transferring each one as it opens to the mussel bowl (if any don't open after 8 minutes, discard them). Strain the cooking liquid through a fine-mesh sieve lined with a double layer of cheesecloth or a coffee filter to remove sand and reserve the liquid separately.

MAKE THE SOUP: In a large pot set over medium heat, heat the remaining 3 tablespoons olive oil and add the scallions, garlic, thyme, and saffron. Season with salt and cook, stirring, until the scallions become tender and the garlic translucent, 5 to 8 minutes. Add the canned tomatoes and fish stock plus 1 cup water. Reduce the heat to low and simmer gently until the flavors meld and the tomato mellows, 20 to 25 minutes. Remove the thyme sprigs and squeeze any excess liquid (and flavor) from them into the soup before discarding.

ASSEMBLE: Shell almost all of the mussels and clams but leave a few in the shells for garnish. Add the clam and mussel cooking liquid to the soup, along with the mussel and clam bodies. Add the mussels and clams in their shells as well. Gently add the fish and heat just until warmed, 2 to 3 minutes. Taste for seasoning and keep warm.

MAKE THE AIOLI: In a medium bowl, whisk the mayonnaise with the garlic, Worcestershire, and Tabasco with a pinch of salt. Gently grate the surface of one of the limes 2 to 3 times to get a hint of the zest. Then juice both limes and add all of the juice.

SERVE: Ladle the soup into bowls and top each serving with a generous dollop of the aioli. Serve with slices of toasted sourdough bread on the side.

HOME
Pasta Doughs, Gnocch

Mastering homemade pasta dough simply takes practice. In this chapter, we explore the topic from classic fresh pastas to gnocchi. And because pasta needs sauce, I've included almost all the tomato sauces I grew up with. Plus, sauces are like moods—ever changing and always exciting. My most recent addition is an uncooked tomato sauce, where the tomatoes are raw and almost grassy and herbaceous.

MADE
Tomato Sauces

PASTA + SAUCE = HAPPINESS

While any pasta can be a match for your favorite sauce if you love the combination, there are some classic shapes and types of pasta that go with the iconic sauces. You can use the shape in fresh (page 96 for fresh pasta dough) or dry form.

penne

farfalle

Mom's Marinara sauce	+	Goes with all pasta shapes
Dad's Marinara	+	Fettuccine
Grandma Guarnaschelli's Marinara	+	Spaghetti with meatballs
Raw tomato sauce	+	Spaghetti
Tomato vodka sauce	+	Penne
Bolognese sauce	+	Bucatini/Tagliatelle
Alfredo sauce	+	Fettuccine
Carbonara sauce	+	Fettuccine
Primavera sauce	+	Farfalle
Arrabbiata sauce	+	Penne
Cacio e Pepe	+	Spaghetti/Bucatini
Pork shoulder (or any meat ragu)	+	Orecchiette/Papardelle
Arugula pesto	+	Rigatoni
Pasta e fagioli	+	Elbows or any small pasta
Squash and sage	+	Cavatappi or Gnocchi

lasagna

ravioli

rigatoni

orecchiette

orzo

PASTA DOUGH

SERVES 6 TO 10, MAKES ABOUT 1 POUND DOUGH

There are a million ways to make pasta dough and I have tried many. But this is the natural recipe that tends to live in my head. I always say if this is what I make under pressure in a competition show, then it's probably the truest recipe I know. I sacrilegiously use it for most types of pasta even though I pretend to have 100 versions of dough, one for each pasta shape. With a name like Guarnaschelli, I have to keep some secrets about the simplicity of my cooking! I hope you make this your simple staple pasta, too. Note that "00" is a fine, powdery flour rich in protein that creates a supple texture, while semolina is a durum wheat flour high in gluten that gives a nice chew and balances the "00" flour.

1¼ cups 00 flour, plus more as needed

⅓ cup plus 2 tablespoons semolina flour

8 large egg yolks, lightly beaten

2 tablespoons extra-virgin olive oil

MIX THE DOUGH: In the bowl of a stand mixer fitted with the paddle attachment, mix the 00 flour and semolina flour. Add the egg yolks, oil, and 3 tablespoons water and mix on medium speed just until the ingredients come together, 3 to 4 minutes.

recipe continues →

PASTA DOUGH *continued*

KNEAD THE DOUGH: Reduce the speed to medium-low and knead the dough until it comes together and feels silky and smooth from all the egg yolks, about 6 to 8 minutes. Add a pinch more flour if the dough sticks or is too wet.

FORM THE DOUGH: The dough can't sit out at room temperature or it gets too mushy to roll because of the richness from all of the egg yolks. Form into a ball, press it flat, and wrap in plastic. To "relax" the dough, refrigerate it for at least 2 hours or up to 12 hours.

GET READY: On a flat, lightly floured surface, cut the dough into four even pieces and let them sit for about 10 minutes to take off the refrigerator chill. Roll slightly with a rolling pin to flatten more.

recipe continues →

ROLL THE DOUGH: Set the rollers on a pasta machine at the biggest/widest setting. Dust the dough with flour and roll one piece of dough through the rollers twice. Move to the next narrower setting and run the dough through twice. Flour the dough and machine lightly as you roll on each setting, making the dough thinner and the pasta sheet larger. At this point, gauge the thickness of the dough based on the pasta shape you're making. Some shapes like lasagna noodles and pappardelle need to be made from slightly thicker sheets, some, like fettuccine and linguine, from thinner ones.

CUT AND STORE THE PASTA: You can cut the pasta, portion it out, and generously flour between the strands to prevent sticking. Store well-wrapped on a floured baking dish in the freezer for up to 24 hours, until ready to drop in boiling water. You can also drape the pasta on a rack to dry overnight, then cook slightly dried depending on the dish you intend to make. You can also use this dough for ravioli or tortellini.

SPINACH PASTA DOUGH

SERVES 6 TO 10; MAKES ABOUT 1¼ POUNDS OF DOUGH

This is a simple recipe, without too many ingredients, and makes a nice dough. While spinach is often watery and kind of tasteless, highlighting it with just flour and a little egg gives it center stage. The spinach has both sour and fresh green notes that really come to the forefront. I admit this recipe is a little equipment heavy, but it's unavoidable. The dough is particularly great with rich sauces and cheeses like ricotta and fontina and makes lovely ravioli.

3 tablespoons extra-virgin olive oil

2 cups tightly packed baby spinach leaves (fully washed and dried, any thick stems removed)

Kosher salt

2 large eggs

2 cups "00" flour, plus more for rolling

COOK THE SPINACH: Heat a large skillet over medium heat and add 1 tablespoon of the olive oil. When the oil is hot and begins to smoke lightly, add the spinach with a pinch salt. Remove the pan from heat and stir with a wooden spoon until the spinach wilts and loses half its volume, 1 to 2 minutes. Transfer to a baking sheet to cool. Place all of the spinach in a kitchen towel and roll it up. Twist the towel gently and squeeze to remove any excess liquid.

MAKE THE SPINACH BASE: In the bowl of the food processor, combine the spinach, eggs, and remaining 2 tablespoons olive oil and process until smooth.

MAKE THE PASTA DOUGH: In the bowl of a stand mixer fitted with the paddle attachment, add the flour. With the machine running on medium speed, add the spinach mixture and mix just until the ingredients come together, 4 to 5 minutes.

KNEAD THE DOUGH: Reduce the speed to medium-low and knead the dough until smooth, 2 to 3 minutes.

FORM THE DOUGH: The dough can't sit out at room temperature, or it gets too mushy to roll because of the richness from all of the egg yolks. Form into a ball, press it flat, and wrap in plastic. To "relax" the dough, refrigerate it for at least 2 hours or up to 12 hours.

GET READY: On a flat, lightly floured surface, cut the dough into four even pieces and let them sit for about 10 minutes to take off the refrigerator chill. Roll slightly with a rolling pin to flatten more.

ROLL THE DOUGH: Set the rollers on a pasta machine at the biggest/widest setting. Dust the dough with flour and roll one piece of dough through the rollers twice. Move to the next narrower setting and again run the dough through the rollers twice. Flour the dough and machine lightly as you roll on each setting, making the dough thinner and the pasta sheet larger. At this point, gauge the thickness of the dough based on the pasta shape you're making. Some shapes like lasagna noodles and pappardelle need to be made from slightly thicker sheets, some, like fettuccine and linguine, from thinner ones.

CUT AND STORE THE PASTA: You can cut the pasta, portion it out, and generously flour it between the strands to prevent sticking. Store well-wrapped on a floured baking sheet in the freezer for up to 24 hours, until ready to drop in boiling water. You can also drape the pasta on a rack to dry overnight, then cook slightly dried depending on the dish you intend to make. You can also use this dough for ravioli or tortellini.

EGGLESS PASTA DOUGH

SERVES 8 TO 10; MAKES ABOUT 1¼ POUNDS DOUGH

This dough relies on the sturdy nature of all-purpose and semolina flours. The richness that a bit of olive oil brings helps make it more cohesive as it mixes. Experiment with using a roasted nut oil (almond or hazelnut, for example) in place of the olive oil if you want. This dough can be a little more chewy since there are no eggs to tenderize it, but it does make a great foundation for tasty vegan dishes, and it especially shines when paired with a hearty sauce loaded with roasted vegetables.

1 cup all-purpose flour, plus more as needed	2 tablespoons extra-virgin olive oil
1 cup semolina flour	1 teaspoon kosher salt

MIX THE DOUGH: In the bowl of a stand mixer fitted with the paddle attachment, mix the all-purpose and semolina flours. With the machine running on medium speed, add ½ cup plus 3 tablespoons water, the olive oil, and salt and mix just until the ingredients come together, 2 to 3 minutes.

KNEAD THE DOUGH: Reduce the speed to medium-low and knead the dough until smooth, 6 to 8 minutes. Add a pinch more flour if the dough sticks as you mix it.

FORM THE DOUGH: The dough can't sit out at room temperature, or it gets too mushy to roll. Form the dough into a ball, press it flat, and wrap in plastic. Refrigerate for at least 2 hours, or up to 12 hours.

GET READY: On a flat, lightly floured surface, cut the dough into four even pieces and let them sit for about 10 minutes to take off the refrigerator chill. Roll slightly with a rolling pin to flatten more.

ROLL THE DOUGH: Set the rollers on a pasta machine at the biggest/widest setting. Dust the dough with flour and roll one piece of dough through the rollers twice. Move to the next narrower setting and again run the dough through the rollers twice. Flour the dough and machine lightly as you roll on each setting, making the dough thinner and the pasta sheet larger. At this point, gauge the thickness of the dough based on the pasta shape you're making. Some shapes like lasagna noodles and pappardelle need to be made from slightly thicker sheets, some, like fettuccine and linguine, from thinner ones.

CUT AND STORE THE PASTA: You can cut the pasta, portion it out, and generously flour it between the strands to prevent sticking. Store well-wrapped on a floured baking sheet in the freezer for up to 24 hours, until ready to drop in boiling water. You can also drape the pasta on a rack to dry overnight, then cook slightly dried depending on the dish you intend to make.

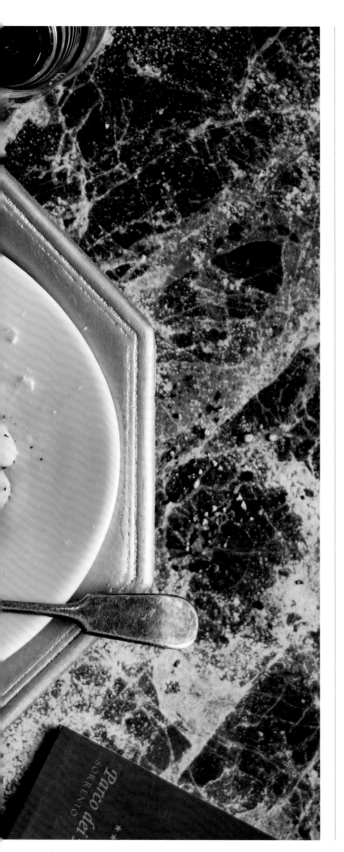

RICOTTA GNOCCHI

SERVES 4 TO 6

These dumplings are lighter than classic potato gnocchi as the ricotta lends richness without making them overly heavy. They are a blank canvas that you can leave fairly simple by saucing with good butter and Pecorino Romano or Parmigiano Reggiano (which will always remind me of childhood buttered noodles). Or amplify them with spices or rich sauces like Mom's Massachusetts Marinara (page 112). Sometimes I'll add some roasted vegetables and fresh herbs to mix it up.

1 pound (16 ounces) whole-milk ricotta cheese

Kosher salt and freshly ground black pepper

2 large egg yolks, lightly beaten

½ cup all-purpose flour, plus more for dusting

¼ teaspoon ground nutmeg

4 tablespoons (½ stick) unsalted butter

½ cup finely grated Parmesan cheese

Juice from 1 large lemon

MAKE THE DOUGH: Spread the ricotta on a baking sheet for easier seasoning. Sprinkle with salt and taste to adjust seasoning, if needed. Drizzle the egg yolks over the ricotta. Combine the flour and nutmeg in a fine-mesh strainer and dust over the ricotta in an even layer (to prevent clumping). Mix gently with a flexible spatula or your hands just until the mixture comes together. Do not overmix or the gnocchi will be tough.

recipe continues →

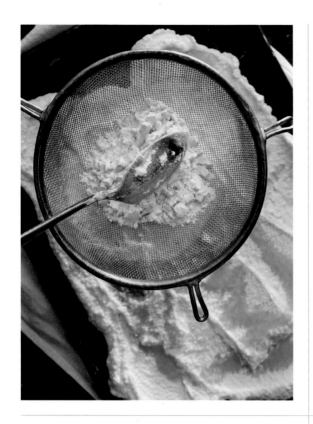

RICOTTA GNOCCHI *continued*

FORM THE GNOCCHI: On a flat, floured surface, divide the dough into four equal portions. Roll each portion into a log about 1 inch in diameter. Using a small knife, cut the dough into 1-inch pieces and roll each piece gently into a ball. Gently press each ball while rolling over the tines of a fork to create ridges on one side. (The ridges allow the gnocchi to catch sauce when finishing the dish.)

BLANCH THE GNOCCHI: Bring a large pot of water to a rolling boil and add a generous handful of salt. The water should taste like seawater. Line a baking sheet with a clean kitchen towel. Add the gnocchi to the boiling water and cook until they float back up to the surface, 1 to 2 minutes. Use a slotted spoon to transfer in a single layer to the kitchen towel to drain.

FINISH: In a large skillet set over medium heat, melt the butter. Add the gnocchi in a single layer. Warm gently, rolling in the butter, until the gnocchi are hot, 2 to 3 minutes. Season with salt and pepper and sprinkle with the Parmesan cheese and lemon juice.

MOM'S MASSACHUSETTS
MARINARA page 112

DAD'S TRIPLE-TOMATO
MARINARA page 113

MOM'S MASSACHUSETTS MARINARA

SERVES 4 TO 6

My mom's family name was DiBenedetto. She grew up in Boston, eating New England blueberries with heavy cream in the summer and at chain restaurants like Friendly's year-round. Her mom, my grandmother, was a real "spitfire" as they say, and she cooked well enough to match her temper. My mom liked her cooking but also loved eating in the Italian restaurants in the Boston area. She said she always liked the subtle sweetness of her mom's tomato sauce and set about making a recipe that created that nostalgic flavor (it's a bonus that it comes together in 30 minutes). Perciatelli or bucatini, both thick spaghetti-like pastas with a hollow core, were her pastas of choice, and they're mine, too. The only person who didn't love her sauce was, ironically, my dad. So you'll find *his* sauce on page 113.

2 tablespoons extra-virgin olive oil

2 small yellow onions, halved and thinly sliced

1 medium carrot, coarsely grated

4 large garlic cloves, grated

Kosher salt

½ teaspoon red pepper flakes

1 (28-ounce) can peeled whole tomatoes

1 teaspoon sugar

Leaves from 5 sprigs fresh basil

MAKE THE SAUCE: In a large skillet set over medium heat, heat the olive oil. Add the onion, carrot, and garlic. Season with salt and the red pepper flakes. Cook, stirring, until the onions become translucent, 5 to 8 minutes. Add the canned tomatoes and sugar. Use a wooden spoon to break up some of the whole tomatoes and cook, stirring from time to time, for 15 minutes. Add about 1 cup water and continue cooking until the tomatoes are broken down and soft, about 10 minutes more. Taste for seasoning and stir in the basil leaves. Store in the refrigerator for up to 2 days, or freeze in batches and defrost as needed.

DAD'S TRIPLE-TOMATO MARINARA

SERVES 4 TO 6

So we know about my mom's sauce (opposite), but my dad's sauce was always a bit of a wild card. He put so many types of tomato products in all of his Italian American dishes that my head would spin. Like tomato paste, which he loved; he'd buy those little cans and stash them like he was hoarding gold. He also bought passata, which is simply pureed and strained tomatoes that are free of bitter seeds and acidic bits of skin. Passata adds body against the tang of the tomato paste and the heartiness of the canned tomatoes. Like my dad's personality, his marinara had many versions of the same ingredients, making both him and his sauce layered and interesting. As for the pasta type, my dad was team dried pasta all the way, and marinara was always made for rigatoni.

- 2 tablespoons extra-virgin olive oil
- 3 medium yellow onions, halved and thinly sliced
- 3 large garlic cloves, grated
- Kosher salt
- 3 tablespoons tomato paste
- 1 (28-ounce) can peeled whole tomatoes
- 1 (12- to 15-ounce) bottle tomato passata
- 1 tablespoon garlic powder
- 1 tablespoon dried oregano
- 2 teaspoons sugar

START THE SAUCE: In a large skillet set over medium heat, heat the olive oil. Add the onion and garlic and season with salt. Cook, stirring, until the onions become translucent, 5 to 8 minutes. Add the tomato paste, raise the heat to medium-high, and fry, stirring, until the paste breaks apart and melds with the onions; you should smell the tartness of the paste as it escapes from the pan. Don't rush this part—let the tomato paste break down; it should take 4 to 5 minutes.

COOK THE SAUCE: Add the canned tomatoes, passata, garlic powder, oregano, sugar, and 2 cups water to the sauce base and reduce the heat to medium. Cook, stirring from time to time, until the tomatoes are broken down, 30 to 35 minutes. Taste for seasoning. At this point, my dad would taste and add a squeeze more of tomato paste or more salt or sugar to amp up the flavors. Store in the refrigerator for up to 2 days, or freeze in batches and defrost as needed.

PS: Can't find passata? Try tomato puree from Pomì. You can also buy and use strained tomatoes from the same brand. Or make your own by pureeing a few ripe tomatoes and straining out the seeds and skin.

GRANDMA GUARNASCHELLI'S MARINARA
WITH BEEF MEATBALLS

SERVES 8 TO 10

I did not have an Italian grandmother who was always around cooking. I only saw Grandma Guarnaschelli on special occasions—so she'd cook everything under the sun to honor my visit. Even as a kid, I was impressed that she went to such trouble. Like rolling and browning little meatballs and layering them throughout lasagna—I remember wondering if they were worth the work. After my first bite, there was little doubt. I've always loved how in a traditional Bolognese sauce, the ground beef and tomato work together so well as a single unit—but I have to admit that there's something equally as wonderful when you get a bit of the beef from a little meatball and then the separate sensation of the tomato sauce that makes the flavors pop even more. The ultimate pairing for Grandma's sauce is fresh fettuccine or tagliatelle (page 96) or a pound of box spaghetti cooked al dente. Toss either with the sauce and then top with the meatballs and grated Parmesan cheese.

MAKE THE SAUCE: In a large, heavy-bottomed pot set over medium heat, heat the olive oil. When it begins to smoke lightly, add the pancetta and cook, stirring, until the meat browns and crisps, 3 to 4 minutes. Remove most of the pancetta with a spatula and drain on paper towels. Add the onions, minced garlic, and red pepper flakes to the pot and season with salt. Cook, stirring, until the onions are translucent, about 5 minutes. Add 2 cups water, the canned tomatoes, and the sugar. Cook over medium heat, stirring from time to time, until the tomatoes fall apart, 20 to 25 minutes. Keep warm.

MAKE THE MEATBALLS: While the sauce is cooking, put the beef in a large bowl, spread it all over the bottom and up the sides a little, and sprinkle with a generous pinch of salt. Sprinkle the Parmesan cheese, breadcrumbs, parsley, and cooked pancetta all over the meat and use your hands to gently mix, just until all of the ingredients mix together. Do not overmix or overwork the meat. In a small bowl, whisk together the egg and grated garlic. Drizzle the mixture over the meat, then mix the meat thoroughly with your hands.

COOK AND TASTE ONE MEATBALL: Roll one small meatball, about ½ inch in diameter. In a large skillet over high heat, heat a splash of the olive oil. When the oil begins to smoke lightly, remove the skillet from the heat. Add the meatball to the skillet, return the pan to the heat and cook, turning as it browns on all sides, until cooked through, 3 to 5 minutes. Taste for seasoning and texture. If too wet, add more breadcrumbs to the meat mixture. If too dry, add another beaten egg. Roll the remaining meat into about 20 balls approximately 2 inches in diameter.

TOMATO SAUCE

- 2 tablespoons extra-virgin olive oil
- ½ cup finely diced pancetta
- 2 medium yellow onions, minced
- 6 large garlic cloves, minced
- ½ teaspoon red pepper flakes
- Kosher salt
- 1 (28-ounce) can peeled whole tomatoes
- 2 teaspoons sugar

MEATBALLS

- 1 pound ground beef (preferably 80% lean sirloin)
- Kosher salt
- ¾ cup finely grated Parmesan cheese
- ½ cup panko breadcrumbs, plus more if needed
- 12 to 14 sprigs fresh curly parsley (stems and all), coarsely chopped
- 1 large egg, lightly beaten, plus more if needed
- 3 large garlic cloves, grated
- ⅓ cup extra-virgin olive oil

COOK THE MEATBALLS: Line a baking sheet with a clean kitchen towel. Heat the same skillet again over high heat and add about half of the remaining olive oil. When the oil begins to smoke lightly, remove the skillet from the heat and add half of the meatballs in a single layer, spreading them somewhat apart so they have a chance to brown instead of steaming. Return the pan to high heat and cook, turning the balls so they brown all around, for 2 to 3 minutes total. The meat should be medium-rare at this point, not cooked through. Use a slotted spoon or spatula to transfer them to the kitchen towel to drain any excess grease. Wipe out the bottom of the skillet and cook the remaining meatballs in the remaining oil.

THE MEATBALL JACUZZI: Return the sauce to a simmer if necessary. Gently lower the meatballs into the simmering sauce "Jacuzzi" and let them cook over medium-low heat for about 5 minutes. Shut off the heat and let the pot rest on the stove for at least 20 minutes. The resting period allows the flavors to develop. You can even make this the night before and reheat for even better results.

RAW TOMATO SAUCE

SERVES 4 TO 6

This recipe is entirely dependent on the quality and ripeness of your tomatoes. Now it's not financial. You don't need to invest your 401(k) in fancy heirlooms to come out ahead here. In fact, I honestly prefer regular Romas or beefsteaks. What is of utmost importance is to buy tomatoes that have great flavor, acidity, and, ideally, are juicy-ripe. If you have some almost overripe ones hanging around, this could be a good way to repurpose them if they're too far gone for BLTs. To add even more horsepower, toss a few sun-dried tomatoes in the blender with everything, if you have a few lying around. I like this sauce with a playful shape like cavatappi or farfalle pasta, or any other shape that traps bits of sauce and has a little tooth to it since the sauce is so smooth.

10 ripe medium Roma tomatoes, cored and halved

½ cup extra-virgin olive oil

3 tablespoons tomato paste

1 teaspoon garlic powder

1 teaspoon dried oregano

1 teaspoon honey

1 teaspoon balsamic vinegar

Kosher salt

MAKE THE SAUCE: In the blender (you may need to blend in batches depending on your blender), combine the tomatoes, olive oil, tomato paste, garlic powder, oregano, honey, balsamic, and a generous pinch of salt. Blend until smooth. Taste for seasoning.

Serve with your pasta of choice, or transfer to an airtight container and store in the refrigerator up to 2 days, or freeze in batches and defrost as needed.

PENNE
WITH VODKA SAUCE

SERVES 6 TO 8

This is a dish with questionable beginnings. Some think it was invented by a college student in New York City in the 1970s or 1980s; some say it originated in Italy; another story speaks of a chef in a restaurant who needed to thin out some tomato sauce and did it with the vodka in a flask from his pocket. No matter its origin story, what we know is that it's a beloved red-sauce restaurant go-to with a bold red-orange hue (which always reminds me of lipstick from the 1980s). Yes, this is made with vodka and some alcohol does remain when you cook with it, but the sauce—with cream, tomato, and vodka all intersecting—just really works and is so balanced. I toss it with rigatoni or penne, but also love it as a dunking sauce for squid (page 71), grilled zucchini (page 53), or even on the side with Gnocchi alla Romana (page 28). Another idea from my kitchen: Spread the sauce on an English muffin and top with mozzarella to make a retro toaster oven pizza. A tip to remember: The cream should be at room temperature so it doesn't separate when mixed into the warm sauce, which can happen with chilled cream.

2 tablespoons extra-virgin olive oil

1 medium yellow onion, minced

2 large garlic cloves, minced

Kosher salt

¼ cup cheap vodka (see PS)

2 teaspoons sugar

¼ teaspoon red pepper flakes

1 (14.5-ounce) can peeled whole tomatoes

¼ cup heavy cream, at room temperature

1 pound penne pasta

Leaves from 4 sprigs fresh basil

MAKE THE SAUCE: In a medium skillet set over medium heat, heat the olive oil. Add the onion and garlic and season with salt. Stir in the vodka, sugar, and red pepper flakes. Cook the vodka down until you can no longer taste "raw" alcohol in the sauce, about 5 minutes. Add the tomatoes, raise the heat to high, and cook, stirring from time to time, until smooth, an additional 5 to 8 minutes. Taste for seasoning. Stir in the cream. Transfer the mixture to a blender and carefully puree until smooth. Serve immediately with pasta, or refrigerate for up to 2 days. Or freeze in batches and defrost as needed.

COOK THE PASTA: In a large pot, bring 4 quarts water to a rolling boil. Add a generous handful of salt; it should be salty like seawater. Add the penne and stir with a slotted spoon to make sure it does not clump or stick to the bottom as it cooks. Cook for 8 to 10 minutes, until al dente. Reserve ½ cup of the pasta cooking liquid, then drain the pasta in a large colander.

ASSEMBLE: Add the hot pasta right from the colander to the skillet and toss to coat with the sauce. Shut the heat off and allow the pasta to rest for 2 minutes. If the sauce is too thin, gently warm and reduce over low heat for 1 to 2 additional minutes. If it is too thick, simply thin it out with some of the reserved pasta cooking liquid. Top with the basil and serve.

PS: I don't subscribe to the point of view that you get a higher quality sauce if you use expensive vodka. I've never been able to taste the nuances of pricey liquor in cooking, except maybe a red wine sauce that just has gently reduced wine and a little butter to finish. I say: Save the expensive stuff for savoring and sipping and use the more affordable ones for cooking.

QUADRUPLE
GARLIC BREAD page 231

CLASSIC
Dishes

When it comes to the classic pasta dishes, everyone seems to have an opinion. Is carbonara made with cream, should an alfredo really include frozen peas, and what constitutes the proper vegetables for a primavera? In this chapter you'll find some answers to these questions with recipes for iconic pasta dishes that should be a part of anyone's repertoire. They're so fun to make, more fun to eat, and the most fun to argue about.

PASTA

1980s DATE-NIGHT
ANGEL HAIR PASTA page 142

CLASSIC SPAGHETTI CARBONARA

SERVES 4 TO 6

This is the classic version of carbonara, in which starchy pasta water combines with egg yolks and the flavors of unctuous pancetta and sharp sheep's milk cheese to get to a seriously tasty place. For an even quicker carbonara, see the cheater's version on page 124.

6 ounces pancetta, finely diced

Kosher salt and freshly ground black pepper

1 pound spaghetti

1 large egg plus 3 large egg yolks, lightly beaten

1 cup finely grated pecorino cheese

2 teaspoons red wine vinegar

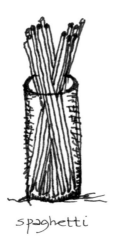

spaghetti

COOK THE PANCETTA: In a large skillet set over medium heat, cook the pancetta, stirring occasionally, until crispy and browned, 3 to 5 minutes. Use a slotted spoon to transfer the pancetta to a large serving bowl, leaving the fat behind.

COOK THE PASTA: Bring a large pot of water to a rolling boil. Add a generous handful of salt. Add the spaghetti and stir with a slotted spoon to make sure it does not clump or stick to the bottom. Cook until al dente, 8 to 10 minutes. Reserve some of the pasta water in case you need it to adjust the texture of your sauce, then drain the pasta in a large colander.

FINISH: Add the egg and yolks and a generous sprinkle of the cheese to the bowl with the pancetta along with some of the cooking grease. Add the pasta with a splash of the cooking water and use a whisk to mix vigorously. The goal is to have both the eggs and cheese link up to coat the pasta. The pasta water is the connector. Keep in mind, the pasta should be a little loose and the sauce will thicken as the pasta cools for just a few minutes. If too thick, loosen with more pasta water. Season with pepper and stir in the vinegar. Taste for seasoning.

SERVE: Spoon the pasta into individual bowls and top with the remaining cheese.

CHEATER'S CARBONARA

SERVES 4 TO 6

Sometimes it's good to cheat a little. Classic carbonara fans insist the dish cannot be made with cream and that all the creaminess must come from the egg yolks and cheese mixed with the starchy pasta water. The name comes from the Italian legend that coal miners were eating this dish and the flecks of pepper mimic the flecks of coal that might have been in the bowls as the "carbones" (coal burners) ate in the mines. Modernists feel adding cream provides a little extra sauciness as well as a security policy that the sauce will nicely coat the pasta. Who am I to argue? I love carbonara both ways but most often turn to the cheater's style because I just like the simplicity of the recipe.

- 6 ounces pancetta, finely diced
- Kosher salt and freshly ground black pepper
- 1 pound spaghetti
- 1 cup heavy cream, warmed
- 1 cup finely grated pecorino cheese
- 2 large egg yolks, lightly beaten
- 2 teaspoons red wine vinegar

COOK THE PANCETTA: In a large skillet set over medium heat, cook the pancetta until crispy and browned, 3 to 5 minutes, stirring occasionally. Drain the pancetta through a fine-mesh sieve and reserve the grease. Transfer the pancetta to a large serving bowl.

COOK THE PASTA: Bring a large pot of water to a rolling boil. Add a generous handful salt. Add the spaghetti and stir with a slotted spoon to make sure it does not clump or stick to the bottom. Cook until al dente, 8 to 10 minutes. Reserve 1 cup of the pasta water in case you need it to adjust the texture of your sauce, then drain the pasta in a large colander.

FINISH: To the bowl with the pancetta, add the cream, a generous sprinkle of the cheese, and the yolks, along with some of the cooking grease. Add the pasta with a splash of the cooking water and use a whisk to vigorously combine. Keep in mind, the pasta will be a little loose and the sauce will thicken as the pasta cools for a few minutes. If too thick, loosen with more pasta water. Season with pepper and stir in the vinegar. Taste for seasoning. Serve in bowls, topped with the remaining cheese.

FETTUCCINE ALFREDO

SERVES 4 TO 6

This dish can be made with dry or fresh fettuccine (I prefer fresh)—but you have to commit to fettuccine. The long, flat noodles soak up the cream and cheese like no other. Slurping it up and needing many napkins is how I see this dish being eaten. Truth is, when you have cream and Parmigiano Reggiano cheese, there is little else required beyond some salt and black pepper. If using fresh pasta, the cook time will be shorter (also, add an extra handful of pasta for this amount of sauce). If possible, grate the Parmigiano right from a block for its super fresh flavor.

4 tablespoons (½ stick) unsalted butter

1 cup heavy cream

Kosher salt and freshly ground black pepper

1 cup finely grated Parmesan cheese, plus more for serving

1 pound fettuccine, dried or fresh

1 cup frozen peas, thawed

MAKE THE SAUCE: In a large skillet set over medium-low heat, melt the butter. Add the cream, gently bring to a simmer, and stir in 1 cup of the Parmesan. Season with salt and pepper and keep warm while you make the pasta. Keep warm.

COOK THE PASTA: Bring a large pot of water to a rolling boil. Add a generous amount of salt; the pasta water should taste like seawater. Add the fettuccine to the pot and stir so it doesn't stick to the bottom. Cook the pasta until al dente, chewy but not hard or raw tasting, 8 to 10 minutes for dried pasta. Reserve a little of the pasta cooking liquid, then drain the pasta in a colander.

COMBINE THE PASTA AND SAUCE: Add the pasta directly to the sauce and toss. The sauce should coat the pasta without being overly thick or clumpy—if it's too thick, thin with a little pasta water. Taste for seasoning. Stir in the peas. Let the pasta rest in the sauce off the heat for 1 to 2 minutes to allow the flavors to integrate. Serve in bowls, topped with additional cheese.

FARFALLE PRIMAVERA

SERVES 4 TO 6

Farfalle or "bow tie" pasta captures sauce in all the crevices. Another nuance of this pasta shape is that the center of the bow tie remains firm when the pasta is cooked, offering an extra bit of "chew." In this primavera, that extra chew pairs so nicely with spring vegetables and stands up to the richness of the creamy sauce. This really isn't an Italian dish as much as a New York City Italian restaurant dish—and even more specifically, a 1970s, retro Italian American New York City dish. Sirio Maccioni of the famed restaurant Le Cirque says his wife tossed together some leftover spring vegetables, cream, and pasta to create this dish, and as a result, it became an off-menu item at his restaurant. If you knew about it, you could order it. If not, well, we can make it here together.

Kosher salt and freshly ground black pepper

12 medium asparagus spears, cut into thin rounds, tips reserved

1 medium head broccoli, cut into small, bite-size florets, stem peeled and cut into thin rounds

2 tablespoons unsalted butter

1 large yellow onion, halved and thinly sliced

2 medium carrots, cut into ¼-inch-thick rounds

1 cup heavy cream

1 tablespoon Worcestershire sauce

1 teaspoon Tabasco sauce

1 pound farfalle

1 cup frozen peas, thawed

Leaves from 2 sprigs fresh basil

BLANCH THE VEGETABLES: Fill a large bowl half full with cold water and ice and place a colander inside it. Bring a large saucepan of water to a rolling boil. Add a generous amount of salt. Add the asparagus to the pot and cook for 2 minutes. Use a slotted spoon to transfer to the colander to cool in the ice water. Cook the broccoli florets and stems the same way for 2 minutes and transfer to the ice bath with the asparagus. Drain the vegetables and pat dry to remove excess moisture.

MAKE THE SAUCE: In a large skillet set over medium heat, melt the butter. Add the onion and carrots and season generously with salt and pepper. Cook, stirring often, until the onions are translucent and tender, 5 to 8 minutes. Add the cream, Worcestershire, and Tabasco and bring to a simmer. Add the broccoli and asparagus and keep warm as the pasta cooks.

COOK THE PASTA: In a large pot, bring 6 quarts of water to a rolling boil. Add a generous handful of salt; the pasta water should taste like seawater. Add the farfalle to the pot and stir so it doesn't stick to the bottom. Cook the pasta until al dente, chewy but not hard or raw tasting, 8 to 10 minutes. Reserve a little of the pasta water, then drain the pasta in a colander.

FINISH: Toss the pasta with the sauce, stir in the peas, and let it rest, off the heat, for 2 to 3 minutes so the sauce cools and thickens slightly and the pasta has an opportunity to absorb some of the sauce as well. Serve in bowls, topped with basil.

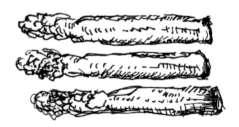

CLASSIC BOLOGNESE

SERVES 6 TO 8

My mother would make iconic Italian sauces and always serve them with bits of lore. Those stories, whether true or accurate, became the thing I knew the dishes by. (And they had to be true because my mother said they were when I was a kid, right?) I am American, obviously, but in these little food moments, we were Italian and I was lost with Mom in a field somewhere in Emilia-Romagna. She told me that a splash of milk at the end of Bolognese could symbolize a family who was wealthy enough to have dairy. She also told me the milk was acidic and sweet to complement the tomato and evoke the sweetness of the starchy pasta. Sometimes I cheat and add heavy cream in its place, but milk makes it more layered and interesting, and, well, it reminds me of Mom.

5 tablespoons extra-virgin olive oil

2 ounces pancetta, finely chopped

1 medium carrot, halved lengthwise and thinly sliced

2 small inner yellow celery stalks, thinly sliced

2 medium shallots, thinly sliced

5 large garlic cloves, minced

1 teaspoon sugar

Kosher salt

1 (28-ounce) can peeled whole tomatoes

1½ pounds ground beef (preferably chuck or a combination of chuck and brisket)

½ teaspoon red pepper flakes

1 cup dry white wine

¼ cup whole milk

1 pound rigatoni pasta

1½ to 2 cups finely grated Parmesan cheese

MAKE THE SAUCE: In a large skillet set over high heat, heat 3 tablespoons of the olive oil. Add the pancetta and cook, stirring, so it browns and crisps, 2 to 3 minutes. Add the carrot, celery, shallots, and garlic. Season with the sugar and a generous pinch of salt. Reduce the heat to medium and cook until the shallots become translucent, 5 to 8 minutes. Add the tomatoes with 2 cups water and simmer over low heat until the tomatoes fall apart, 20 to 25 minutes.

COOK THE BEEF: Meanwhile, heat another large skillet over medium heat and add the remaining 2 tablespoons olive oil. When the oil begins to smoke lightly, add the ground beef in a single layer and season generously with salt. Brown the meat for 5 to 7 minutes, then stir in the red pepper flakes. Stir in the white wine and simmer until the wine cooks out and melds with the beef, 5 to 8 minutes. Taste for seasoning. Pour the tomato sauce over the ground beef. Stir to blend. Simmer over medium heat for about 5 minutes. Shut off the heat, stir in the milk, and allow the sauce to rest.

COOK THE PASTA: Bring a large pot of water to a rolling boil and add 2 tablespoons salt. Add the rigatoni and stir with a slotted spoon to make sure it does not clump or stick to the bottom. Cook for 8 to 10 minutes, until al dente. Reserve some of the cooking liquid in case you need it to adjust the thickness of your sauce, then drain the pasta in a large colander.

COMBINE THE PASTA AND SAUCE: Toss the pasta in the skillet with the Bolognese and add half of the Parmesan cheese. Stir gently, coating the pasta with the sauce (add a splash of pasta water if needed). Warm a little over low heat if it's not piping hot. Serve in individual bowls with the remaining cheese on the side for sprinkling.

CLASSIC PENNE ARRABBIATA

SERVES 6 TO 8

Arrabbiata simply means "angry" and red pepper flakes are certainly the ingredient that expresses that emotion. This is a dish that takes you to the streets of Rome and, in fact, any food cooked with an excess of chiles and garlic is referred to as "arrabbiato," so this pasta represents a whole Italian mood. I enjoy the blunt heat the sauce offers without much else to complement or obstruct it. No herbs or vinegar. Just chili flakes and tomato.

3 tablespoons extra-virgin olive oil

2 medium yellow onions, finely diced

4 large garlic cloves, minced

Kosher salt

2 teaspoons sugar

1 teaspoon red pepper flakes (or less depending on your mood)

1 (28-ounce) can peeled whole tomatoes

1 pound penne pasta

1 cup finely grated Parmesan cheese

MAKE THE SAUCE: In a large skillet set over medium heat, heat the olive oil. Add the onions and garlic, season with salt, then stir in the sugar and red pepper flakes. Cook, stirring from time to time, until the onions become translucent, 3 to 5 minutes. Add the tomatoes and cook, stirring from time to time and crushing the tomatoes with a wooden spoon as they soften and cook, for 15 to 20 minutes.

COOK THE PASTA: In a large pot, bring 4 quarts of water to a rolling boil. Add a generous handful of salt; the pasta water should taste like seawater. Add the pasta and stir with a slotted spoon to make sure it does not clump or stick to the bottom. Cook until al dente, 8 to 10 minutes. Reserve ½ cup of the pasta water then drain the pasta in a large colander.

COMBINE THE PASTA AND SAUCE: Add the hot pasta right from the colander to the skillet and toss to coat with the sauce. Shut the heat off and allow the pasta to rest in the sauce for 6 to 8 minutes. The sauce should coat the pasta easily and resting will allow the flavors to absorb more before eating; if it's too thin, gently warm and reduce over low heat for 1 to 2 additional minutes. If it becomes too thick, simply thin it out with some of the reserved pasta cooking liquid. Serve in bowls, topped with the Parmesan.

DAILY

ASAGNE EGG	4.75
PINACH NOODLES	5.25
LUTEN MACARONI	3.25
APPELLETTI	7.75
AVATELLI	4.75
AVATELLI EGG	4.99
ETTUCCINE	4.75
GNOLOTTI	7.99

Please
WEAR
FACE
MASK

Thank You

On Grand Street in Little Italy at Piemonte Ravioli.

CACIO E PEPE

·

SERVES 4 TO 6

This is a classic, straight-from-the-streets-of-Rome pasta. Cacio e pepe translates as "cheese and pepper" and those two ingredients are the driving force behind this simple, addictive dish. You can enlist any pasta shape, though a long noodle is most traditionally used, like spaghetti or bucatini. The latter is hollow, like a straw, which adds to the heartiness of the pasta and is part of the equation. You want there to be enough cracked pepper that you can taste both the floral notes and the heat as you chew. And while Parmesan cheese may seem the logical ingredient, Pecorino Romano is the classic; its saltiness really amps up the pepper notes. Note that the pasta sauce is solely the pasta cooking liquid and cheese coming together with the pepper—it's all you need for a complete, simple, and tasty dish.

1 tablespoon whole black peppercorns
Kosher salt

1 pound spaghetti
1 cup finely grated pecorino cheese, plus more for serving

CRUSH THE PEPPER: Place the peppercorns on a flat surface. Use the bottom of a small skillet or pot to crush the peppercorns a few times. The pepper will break apart but will be coarser than if ground with the peppermill. Gather it all into a large bowl.

COOK THE PASTA: Bring a large pot of water to a rolling boil and add a generous handful of salt; the pasta water should taste like seawater. Add the spaghetti and stir with a slotted spoon to make sure it does not clump or stick to the bottom. Cook until al dente, 8 to 10 minutes. Reserve 1 cup of the pasta water, then drain the pasta in a large colander.

COMBINE THE PASTA AND CHEESE: Add the pasta to the bowl with the pepper. Sprinkle with about one-third of the cheese and about ½ cup pasta water. Mix vigorously with tongs. Add the remaining cheese and ¼ cup of the pasta water and keep tossing. It should almost look like butter was used to make the sauce and you should smell the pepper and cheese. Serve in bowls, topped with additional cheese.

BAKED ZITI

SERVES 6 TO 8

Ziti is all about cheese, and I don't accept a ziti that isn't excessive. You can assemble this ahead of time and bake when you are ready to eat. I use Parmesan here because the natural salt brings out the sweet and almost creamy notes of the mozzarella. They really go hand in hand. You can make it with rigatoni, just don't tell any Italians about it!

3 tablespoons extra-virgin olive oil

2 medium yellow onions, minced

10 large garlic cloves, minced

Kosher salt

½ teaspoon red pepper flakes

1 (28-ounce) can peeled whole tomatoes

2 teaspoons sugar

2 teaspoons dried oregano

1 pound ziti

1½ pounds whole-milk mozzarella cheese, shredded

2 cups finely grated Parmesan cheese

8 sprigs fresh basil, stemmed

MAKE THE SAUCE: In a large skillet set over medium heat, heat the olive oil. Add the onions and garlic and season with salt and the red pepper flakes. Cook, stirring from time to time, until the onions become translucent, 3 to 5 minutes. Add the tomatoes, sugar, and oregano and stir to blend. Cook, continuing to stir from time to time, until the tomatoes start to smell cooked and the raw garlic mellows, 18 to 20 minutes more. Taste for seasoning.

COOK THE PASTA: Bring a large pot of water to a rolling boil. Add a generous handful of salt; the pasta water should taste like seawater. Add the pasta and stir with a slotted spoon to make sure it does not clump or stick to the bottom. Cook until al dente, 8 to 10 minutes. Reserve ½ cup of the pasta water, then drain the pasta in a large colander.

Preheat the oven to 375°F.

COMBINE THE PASTA AND SAUCE: Add the hot pasta right from the colander to the skillet and toss to coat with the sauce. Shut the heat off and allow the pasta to rest for 10 minutes—ideally the pasta is nicely coated with the sauce but it still looks saucy and not dried out. If it becomes too thick, simply thin it out with some of the reserved pasta water.

BAKE THE PASTA: Fill an 8½ × 11-inch baking dish with half of the ziti, sprinkling half of the mozzarella and Parmesan over the pasta as you fill the dish. Top with all of the remaining pasta and cheese. Bake until the top browns, 15 to 18 minutes. Switch the oven to broil and broil the ziti until the top is browned and the sauce bubbling, 2 to 3 minutes.

SERVE: Tear the basil and sprinkle over the top. Serve family style.

PORK SHOULDER RAGÙ page 140

PORK SHOULDER RAGÙ

SERVES 6 TO 8

This is a typical Italian American Sunday afternoon dish that might be made on a rainy day. If you can, roast the pork the day before, refrigerate, and reheat the next day for even better results. Pork shoulder has some intramuscular fat, which makes it inherently juicy, but it's also possible to overcook the meat—that's where the sauce comes in, because it insulates the meat from drying out. The cooking time can vary a little, and you have to use a little bit of instinct with the meat's doneness, the goal always being fork tender, coated with sauce, and juicy. I put this right over cooked orecchiette (aka "little ears"), but tagliatelle is great, too. It could also easily go over a simple risotto or alongside Ricotta Gnocchi (page 105). The flavors are bold, so the accompanying counterpoint should be mellow.

1 (3-pound) piece boneless pork shoulder

Kosher salt and freshly ground black pepper

1 tablespoon extra-virgin olive oil

¼ pound (4 ounces) pancetta, diced small

3 medium yellow onions, halved and thinly sliced

6 large garlic cloves, thinly sliced

½ teaspoon red pepper flakes

3 cups dry white wine

1 (28-ounce) can peeled whole tomatoes

4 anchovy fillets, coarsely chopped

1 tablespoon fish sauce

2 pints cherry tomatoes, stemmed

1 pound dry orecchiette pasta

2 tablespoons unsalted butter

3 sprigs fresh basil, stemmed

Preheat the oven to 350°F. Position a rack in the center of the oven.

ROAST THE PORK: Season the pork with salt and pepper. Place on a rimmed baking sheet with a fitted rack (to optimize browning). In the center of the oven and roast until the pork is tender and juicy, about 1½ hours. Remove from the oven and allow it to rest 15 minutes.

MAKE THE SAUCE: Heat a Dutch oven over medium-high heat. Add the olive oil and pancetta and cook, stirring occasionally, until browned, 3 to 5 minutes. Add the onions, garlic, and red pepper flakes. Season with salt and cook, stirring from time to time, until the onions are translucent, 8 to 10 minutes. Add the white wine, reduce the heat to medium, and cook until almost all of the liquid cooks off, 8 to 10 minutes. Stir in the canned tomatoes with the anchovy fillets, fish sauce, and 3 cups water. Adjust the heat so the sauce simmers and cook until the tomatoes cook down, 25 to 30 minutes.

FINISH THE MEAT: Lower the pork into the sauce and spoon sauce over the meat to baste it. Add the cherry tomatoes. Cover and gently simmer over low heat, basting from time to time, until cooked through, 15 to 20 minutes. Shut off the heat and let the meat rest 15 minutes.

COOK THE PASTA: Bring a large pot of water to a rolling boil. Add a generous handful of salt; the pasta water should taste like sea water. Add the pasta and stir with a slotted spoon to make sure it does not clump or stick to the bottom. Cook until al dente, 10 to 12 minutes. Reserve ½ cup of the pasta water, then drain the pasta in a large colander. Toss the pasta with 2 tablespoons of the pasta cooking water, the butter and salt and pepper until the butter melts into the pasta.

SERVE: Taste the ragu for seasoning, then tear the basil leaves and stir them into the pasta. Break apart the meat with a spoon and serve in bowls over pasta.

PASTA E FAGIOLI

SERVES 4 TO 6

This is a simple dish that gets a slight tweak or change depending on which region of Italy you are in (or from). In some areas, the dish is interpreted almost as a bean soup. In the south, for example, in Bari (where my father's family is from), a variety of pasta shapes and pancetta make their way into the recipe; the result is a thicker and heartier consistency. In Rome, "pasta e ceci" interprets this dish with chickpeas in place of the beans; the chickpeas give the soup/stew a nuttier flavor profile. Broadly speaking, pasta e fagioli translates to "pasta and beans," and this dish lives somewhere between being a soup and a stew. Truth is, I like to keep it somewhat closer to the soupier side with the understanding that the starches from the pasta and beans naturally create a hearty (but not heavy) texture that makes this the ultimate comfort food. The macaroni is cooked right in the broth so the starches don't get rinsed down the drain but simply gather steam with the white beans and lima beans.

MAKE THE SOUP: In a large pot with a fitted lid, heat the olive oil over medium heat. Add the onion, carrot, celery, garlic, and thyme. Season generously with salt and pepper and cook, stirring from time to time, until the onions are translucent and tender, 5 to 8 minutes. Add the tomatoes and simmer to soften the tomatoes, 5 to 8 minutes, stirring occasionally. Add the chicken stock and cannellini beans and simmer for 2 to 3 minutes. Add the macaroni, cover, and cook until tender, 5 to 6 minutes. At this point, you can see the various starches from the pasta building and adding some texture and body to the broth.

FINISH: Adjust the heat so the soup is gently simmering and add the escarole and green beans. Reduce the heat to medium-low and let the greens wilt and cook, 2 to 3 minutes. Shut off the heat and add the lima beans and cheese. Taste for seasoning and serve with a loaf of crusty bread.

- 2 tablespoons extra-virgin olive oil
- 1 medium yellow onion, finely diced
- 1 medium carrot, cut into thin rounds
- 2 medium stalks celery, peeled and cut into thin rounds
- 2 large garlic cloves, minced
- 2 sprigs fresh thyme
- Kosher salt and freshly ground black pepper
- 1 (14-ounce) can peeled whole tomatoes
- 2 cups chicken stock
- 1 (15-ounce) can cannellini or Great Northern beans, rinsed and drained
- 1 cup elbow macaroni
- 2 cups chopped escarole (bite-size pieces)
- 1 cup chopped green beans (1-inch pieces)
- 1 cup frozen lima beans, thawed
- ¾ cup finely grated pecorino cheese
- Crusty bread, for serving

1980s DATE-NIGHT ANGEL HAIR PASTA

In the 1980s, angel hair pasta with tomatoes was the *it* date dish, and if you were running a restaurant, you had to have it on your menu. Angel hair, or its close (and ever-so-slightly thicker) cousin capellini, is a very thin, fine pasta. It's the pasta that most closely resembles your grandmother's china or those wine glasses on the top shelf that your parents never wanted you to touch. Unlike any other pasta type, angel hair cooks in just a few short minutes and can turn mushy in the blink of an eye, so you must watch it as it cooks. I ate almost exactly this dish a few times in college when on a date with my crush. The servers moved around the dining room on roller skates (all night in roller skates!) and the pasta was always served in a dark blue bowl with a confetti pastel pattern on the edges. The taste? Tomatoes with hints of cream and basil and the glorious texture of the pasta. No cheese. Just nostalgia.

2 tablespoons extra-virgin olive oil

3 large garlic cloves, grated

¼ cup dry white wine

Kosher salt

⅓ cup tomato paste

1 pint cherry tomatoes, halved

1 cup heavy cream

1 pound angel hair pasta

3 sprigs fresh basil, stemmed

MAKE THE SAUCE: In a large skillet, warm the olive oil and garlic over medium heat. Add the white wine and a pinch of salt. Simmer until the liquid cooks out and the garlic becomes tender, 3 to 5 minutes. Stir in the tomato paste with 2 tablespoons water and cook, stirring, to "fry" the paste for a minute in the oil. Add the cherry tomatoes and cook until they soften, 1 to 2 minutes. Add the cream and stir to mix. Season with salt to taste. Keep warm over low heat.

COOK THE PASTA: In a large pot, bring 4 quarts of water to a rolling boil. Add a generous handful of salt; the pasta water should taste like seawater. Add the pasta and stir with a slotted spoon to make sure it does not clump or stick to the bottom. Cook until al dente, 3 to 4 minutes. Reserve ½ cup of the pasta water, then drain the pasta in a large colander.

COMBINE THE PASTA AND SAUCE: Add the hot pasta right from the colander to the skillet and toss to coat with the sauce. Shut the heat off and allow the pasta to rest for 5 to 8 minutes so the pasta absorbs the sauce. If the sauce is too thin, gently warm the pasta over low heat for 1 minute; if it is too thick, simply thin it out with some of the reserved pasta cooking liquid. Tear and add the basil.

SERVE: Twirl a portion of the pasta on a serving fork and gently slip it off onto the center of a plate so it's like a little pasta hill. Roller skates optional.

angel hair

ARUGULA-PESTO PASTA SALAD

SERVES 4 TO 6

There is nothing more tasty and Italian American than the pairing of floral basil and the nutty sweetness of pine nuts with salty cheese and pasta. That said, I think the peppery bite of arugula and the richness of walnuts offer a slight twist to the traditional pesto that elevates this pesto pasta salad. I love the Italian deli staple, but when I make it at home I can salt it as I like and add little touches (like the arugula), which make it more special. I keep this in the fridge as a staple for snacks or quick lunches, but it doesn't hang around long. I love pecorino for the extra burst of salt; you could also add lemon zest to make it slightly brighter and add a citrus note when pairing with fish dishes.

PESTO

Kosher salt

8 sprigs basil, stemmed

2½ cups fresh arugula leaves, packed coarsely chopped

¼ cup walnut halves, coarsely chopped

1 large garlic clove, minced

Freshly ground black pepper

⅓ cup extra-virgin olive oil

PASTA SALAD

1 pound rigatoni

½ cup finely grated pecorino cheese

MAKE THE PESTO: Bring a medium pot of water to a rolling boil. Fill a medium bowl with ice water. Add a generous handful salt to the boiling water, then the basil leaves, and stir. Cook for 1 minute, remove the basil with a slotted spoon, and immediately plunge them into the ice bath to cool, 3 to 5 minutes. Drain the leaves, transfer to a blender, and add three-quarters of the arugula, the walnuts, garlic, salt, freshly ground black pepper, and 2 tablespoons water; blend a little just to combine. With the blender running, slowly stream in the olive oil through the top until somewhat smooth. Transfer the pesto to a large bowl and stir in the remaining arugula.

COOK THE PASTA: Bring a large pot of water to a rolling boil. Add a generous handful of salt; the pasta water should taste like seawater. Add the pasta and stir with a slotted spoon to make sure it does not clump or stick to the bottom. Cook until al dente, 8 to 10 minutes. In a large colander, thoroughly drain the pasta.

COMBINE THE PASTA AND PESTO: Add the hot pasta right from the colander to the bowl and toss to coat with the sauce. Cool at room temperature for 10 minutes, then refrigerate for at least 2 hours, or up to 24 hours. Toss with the cheese just before serving.

BUTTERNUT SQUASH & SAGE PASTA

SERVES 4 TO 6

This is a such a classic Italian fall and winter dish. The almost-minty sage brings out the natural sweetness of hearty butternut squash. (Honeynut, kuri, and kabocha squash work in this recipe as well.) Be careful when cutting squash open—use a large knife and leverage and push right down the center, then keep your hands out of the way as you slice through. (Or buy precut squash and roast in the same way.) I chose farfalle for this because I like its chewy center and the way it traps sage and walnuts in the crevices.

8 tablespoons (1 stick) unsalted butter

Leaves from 4 sprigs fresh sage

½ cup walnut halves

Kosher salt and freshly ground black pepper

3 medium butternut squash (about 2 pounds total)

2 tablespoons dark brown sugar, plus more as needed

2 tablespoons molasses

½ teaspoon ground ginger

½ teaspoon ground cinnamon

¼ teaspoon ground cloves

Zest and juice of 1 medium orange

¼ cup heavy cream

1 pound farfalle

Preheat the oven to 375°F. Position a rack in the center of the oven.

FRY THE SAGE AND WALNUTS: In a small saucepan, melt the butter over medium heat. Add the sage and fry gently until the leaves turn a darker brown and feel somewhat firm to the touch, 2 to 3 minutes. Use a slotted spoon to transfer the leaves to a kitchen towel to drain. Add the walnuts to the butter and fry gently, until they turn slightly darker in color, 2 to 3 minutes. Transfer with a slotted spoon to the sage leaves and season with salt. Continue cooking the butter over medium-low heat until it turns light brown, another 2 to 3 minutes. Remove from the heat and cover to keep warm.

PREPARE THE SQUASH: Place the squash on a flat surface and cut each in half lengthwise. Scrape out the seeds and discard. Arrange the halves cut side up and in a single layer on a baking sheet, season with salt and pepper, and sprinkle with the brown sugar and molasses. Finish by combining the ginger, cinnamon, and cloves in a small fine-mesh strainer and using it to dust the squash with an even layer of the spices. Spoon the brown butter over the squash. Fill the bottom of the baking sheet with about ½ inch water to create steam while the squash cooks. Cover the sheet with aluminum foil and seal the edges tightly.

ROAST THE SQUASH: Place the baking sheet in the center of the oven and bake, undisturbed, for 1½ hours. Pierce the squash with the tip of a small knife; it should be yielding and tender. If not, roast for 30 minutes more. Carefully peel back the foil and let cool.

PUREE THE SQUASH: Using a large spoon, scoop the flesh from the squash, taking care not to take any skin with it. Transfer to a blender. Add a few light grates of orange zest, then cut the orange in half and squeeze in all of the juice. Add the cream and puree until smooth. Pour the puree into a large sauté pan and season with salt and pepper. Cook gently over medium heat, whisking from time to time, to remove any excess water and intensify the flavor, 5 to 8 minutes.

COOK THE PASTA: Bring a large pot of water to a rolling boil. Add a generous amount of salt; the pasta water should taste like seawater. Add the farfalle and stir so it doesn't stick to the bottom. Cook the pasta until al dente, chewy but not hard or raw tasting, 8 to 10 minutes. Reserve a little of the pasta water, then drain the pasta in a colander.

COMBINE THE PASTA AND SAUCE: Add the pasta to the sauce and toss to combine. Taste for seasoning. Sometimes I add a pinch more salt, pepper, and a little more brown sugar to amplify the flavors; add some pasta water if the sauce needs to be thinned.

SERVE: Spoon the pasta and sauce into individual bowls and top with the fried walnuts and sage.

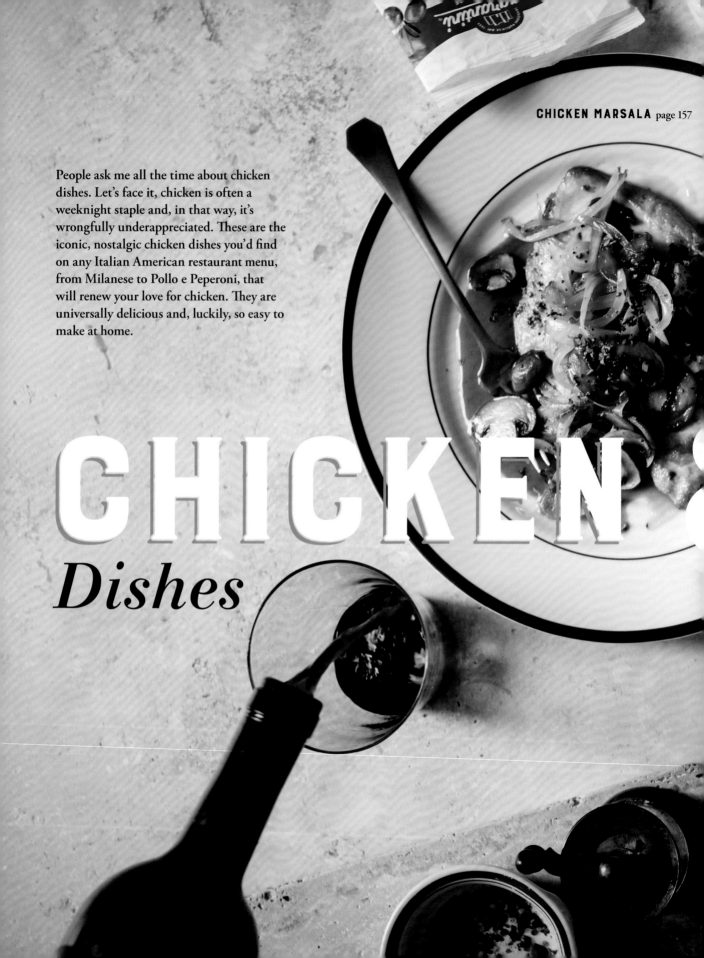

CHICKEN MARSALA page 157

People ask me all the time about chicken dishes. Let's face it, chicken is often a weeknight staple and, in that way, it's wrongfully underappreciated. These are the iconic, nostalgic chicken dishes you'd find on any Italian American restaurant menu, from Milanese to Pollo e Peperoni, that will renew your love for chicken. They are universally delicious and, luckily, so easy to make at home.

CHICKEN
Dishes

POULTRY

BAKED CHICKEN CACCIATORE

●

SERVES 6 TO 8

Cacciatore translates as "hunter's style," and while the tomatoes and garlic don't necessarily tell that whole story, the mushrooms and all the flavors they bring out in the chicken do. It's a classic stovetop red sauce dish, but here I am aiming for more of that oven-baked flavor. I think tomato sauce gets a deeper flavor when it starts on the stove and then is finished in the oven (it reminds me a little of Baked Ziti, page 136).

2 tablespoons extra-virgin olive oil

1 (3½- to 4-pound) whole chicken, cut into 8 parts (breasts halved, thighs, and drumsticks; freeze the wings for another use)

Kosher salt

¼ teaspoon red pepper flakes

2 medium yellow onions, halved and thinly sliced

10 to 12 medium white button mushrooms (8 ounces total), thinly sliced

6 large garlic cloves, thinly sliced

1 cup dry white wine

2 dried bay leaves

1 (28-ounce) can plus 1 (14-ounce) can peeled whole tomatoes

2 teaspoons sugar

4 sprigs fresh thyme

½ cup finely grated Parmesan cheese

4 sprigs fresh basil, stemmed

BROWN THE CHICKEN: Heat a large skillet over high heat, then add the olive oil. Arrange the chicken on a baking sheet in a single layer and season with salt and half the pepper flakes. Turn the pieces on their other side and season again with salt and the remaining pepper flakes. When the oil begins to smoke lightly, use a pair of metal tongs to carefully add the pieces, skin side down, to the oil. Do not overcrowd the pan; you may need to work in batches. Resist the temptation to move or turn the pieces. Reduce the heat to medium and allow them to deeply brown on their first sides, 5 to 8 minutes. Turn the chicken pieces onto their second sides and brown for an additional 5 to 8 minutes. Transfer the chicken to a 9 x 12- or 14-inch baking dish.

Preheat the oven to 375°F. Position a rack in the center of the oven.

MAKE THE SAUCE: To the same skillet, add the onions, mushrooms, and garlic and season with salt. Cook over medium heat, stirring frequently, until the vegetables become tender and release excess liquid, 5 to 8 minutes. Add the white wine and bay leaves and simmer to reduce until almost all the liquid is gone, 5 to 8 minutes. Add the tomatoes and sugar, bring to a simmer, and add the thyme sprigs.

BAKE THE CHICKEN AND SAUCE: Spoon the tomato sauce over the top of the chicken pieces. Bake, uncovered, in the center of the oven until bubbling and hot, 20 to 25 minutes. The chicken should reach an internal temperature of 165°F. Allow the chicken to rest for about 10 minutes. Remove and discard the thyme sprigs and bay leaves. Taste for seasoning, top with the cheese and basil, and serve family style.

CHICKEN MILANESE

SERVES 4

This is the Italian chicken equivalent of a "mother sauce" in French cooking. A breaded chicken cutlet can be taken in so many directions: from a sandwich with a vinegary iceberg salad on the side, to a fancy dinner dish with Meyer lemon and caviar. You can also use this technique with thin slices of veal like my mom did. (Sorry, Mom, but I think chicken is more tender and delicious.) The fillets are also tasty sunken into the layers of a chicken parm (page 159). Some say umami comes from certain ingredients and flavors. I will argue it also comes from certain textures like a crunchy, breaded cutlet.

3 large eggs

2 cups panko breadcrumbs

¼ cup finely grated Parmesan cheese

1 pound or 4 (4-ounce) boneless, skinless chicken breasts, sliced horizontally ¼ inch thick, and then pounded even thinner

Kosher salt

3 tablespoons extra-virgin olive oil

2 tablespoons unsalted butter

4 medium Roma tomatoes, diced

15 fresh basil leaves

Juice from 1 large lemon

BREAD THE CHICKEN: Add the eggs to a small bowl. Add a splash of cold water and whisk to blend. In another medium bowl, combine the breadcrumbs and cheese. Season the chicken pieces on both sides with salt and dip each thoroughly in the eggs and then in breadcrumbs to coat. Place the chicken in a single layer on a baking sheet. Refrigerate for at least 1 hour, or up to 4 hours.

COOK THE CHICKEN: Line a baking sheet with paper towels. In a large skillet set over medium heat, heat half of the olive oil and half of the butter until the butter begins to froth. Add half of the chicken pieces in a single layer and raise the heat to medium-high. Cook until golden brown, 5 to 8 minutes. Use a slotted metal spatula to gently turn them onto their second sides and cook an additional 3 to 5 minutes, until cooked through and no longer opaque. Transfer to the paper towels to drain slightly. Season with salt. Use a paper towel to wipe the skillet free of any excess crumbs. Fry the remaining cutlets in the same way.

FINISH: Remove the excess grease from the skillet and add the tomatoes with a pinch of salt. Increase the heat to medium-high and cook until the tomatoes are warmed through, 1 minute, then add the basil leaves. Transfer the chicken to a serving platter and serve with the tomatoes and the juice from the lemon.

CHICKEN FRANCESE

SERVES 4

This is a pure chicken and lemon dish minus any of the usual suspects like onions, garlic, and even tomatoes—it's one of my daughter's favorites, too. The simplicity of this version leaves you with a few pure (but intense) flavors, including the taste of the chicken itself. Ava and I like to keep it simple and find it more delicious this way. Sometimes we whip up a salad or some greens to go with it. It also pairs nicely with any pasta dish and is also excellent with rice or green beans.

1 pound or 4 (4-ounce) boneless, skinless chicken breasts, sliced horizontally ¼ inch thick, then pounded to be even thinner

Kosher salt and freshly ground black pepper

2 tablespoons extra-virgin olive oil

1 large lemon

½ cup dry white wine

2 tablespoons unsalted butter

1 tablespoon all-purpose flour

COOK THE CHICKEN: Season the chicken cutlets on both sides with salt and pepper. Heat a large skillet over medium heat and add the olive oil. When it begins to smoke lightly, remove the pan from the heat and use a pair of metal tongs to arrange the cutlets in a single layer in the pan. Return the pan to the heat and cook until browned, 3 to 5 minutes. Turn the chicken onto the second sides and cook for 5 to 7 minutes more. Remove the chicken and arrange on a baking sheet to rest while you build the sauce.

MAKE THE SAUCE: Cut a few thin rounds from the lemon and then cut the remainder of the lemon in half; set aside. In the pan where you cooked the chicken, add the white wine and reduce over medium heat until there are just a couple tablespoons of wine remaining, 3 to 5 minutes. Add 2 tablespoons water. In a small bowl, combine the butter and flour, and then whisk into the sauce. Simmer over medium heat, whisking, until smooth. Squeeze in the lemon juice from the two halves. Taste the sauce for seasoning.

FINISH: Add the chicken and any juices from the baking sheet to the sauce and warm gently, basting with the sauce. Add the lemon rounds. Transfer the chicken and lemon to a serving platter and top with the pan sauce.

CHICKEN CUTLETS "SALTIMBOCCA"
WITH PROSCIUTTO & SAGE

SERVES 4 TO 6

While traditional saltimbocca doesn't call for breading the cutlets, there is something irresistible to me about a breaded cutlet, so that's how I make this dish. I also like the way the crunchy layer of breadcrumbs cushions the salt of the prosciutto and mellows the pine notes of the sage. You can certainly make this without the breading, but I don't think you should. The vinegar and lemon juice balance the flavors of this dish.

1 pound or 4 (4-ounce) boneless, skinless chicken breasts, sliced horizontally ¼ inch thick, then pounded even thinner

Kosher salt

3 large eggs

2 to 2½ cups panko breadcrumbs, as needed

8 tablespoons extra-virgin olive oil

8 to 10 slices prosciutto (3½ to 4 ounces)

24 to 30 fresh sage leaves

2 large garlic cloves, thinly sliced

1 tablespoon red wine vinegar

Juice from 1 lemon

PREPARE THE CUTLETS: Line a baking sheet with parchment paper. Season both sides of the chicken cutlets with salt. Lightly beat the eggs in a medium bowl and spread 2 cups breadcrumbs in another. Dip each piece of chicken in the eggs (on both sides) and then in the breadcrumbs to coat. Shake any excess off each one. Add more breadcrumbs if you run low while you're breading. Arrange the cutlets on the baking sheet. Refrigerate for at least 20 minutes, or up to 4 hours.

COOK THE SAGE AND PROSCIUTTO: Preheat the oven to 350°F. In a large skillet, heat 3 tablespoons of the olive oil over low heat. Tear two of the prosciutto slices into small pieces and add to the oil in the pan. Pan-fry over low heat until crispy, 2 minutes, then transfer with a slotted spoon to a plate. Add the sage leaves to the skillet and cook until

they pale in color and become crispy, 2 minutes. Transfer to the plate with the prosciutto and season with salt. With the heat off, stir the garlic into the cooking oil and season with salt. Add another tablespoon olive oil here if the pan is dry. Allow the garlic to simmer in the warm oil for 1 to 2 minutes to cook off the raw flavor, then transfer the garlic and oil to a medium bowl.

WRAP THE CHICKEN: Wrap each piece of chicken around the center with a piece of prosciutto. The prosciutto should naturally stick to the breaded chicken (add part or all of another prosciutto slice if it doesn't completely wrap around the chicken). Arrange in a single layer on a baking sheet.

COOK THE CHICKEN CUTLETS: Line another baking sheet with parchment paper. In a large skillet set over medium heat, heat 3 tablespoons of the olive oil until it smokes lightly. Add the chicken cutlets in a single layer and cook on their first sides until golden brown, 3 to 5 minutes. Turn onto their second sides and cook for an additional 5 to 7 minutes, until the chicken is cooked through and no longer opaque. Transfer the cutlets to the lined baking sheet to drain excess grease and season with salt. Place the baking sheet in the oven to keep warm.

MAKE THE VINAIGRETTE: In a small bowl, whisk the red wine vinegar and lemon juice into the bowl with the reserved garlic and 2 tablespoons olive oil.

SERVE: Arrange the cutlets on a serving platter and drizzle with the vinaigrette. Top with the sage leaves and crispy prosciutto. Serve family style.

PS: Serve the saltimbocca on soft, cushy rolls for a next-level sandwich.

CHICKEN MARSALA

SERVES 4

Marsala wine might be my favorite cooking liquid of all time. It's dry and acidic, but it also has a deeper, almost woodsy note, like bourbon or rye. I don't cook with the fancy stuff—save that for sipping over ice—but just the cheaper stuff you can find in the supermarket. Marsala can be sweet, but for this dish you want a dry Marsala (you can also substitute dry sherry). Take care to reduce the wine so there are no raw alcohol flavors in the finished sauce. This dish is so simple; there aren't many ingredients to hide behind.

1 pound or 4 (4-ounce) boneless, skinless chicken breasts, sliced horizontally ¼ inch thick, then pounded even thinner

Kosher salt

4 tablespoons extra-virgin olive oil

12 ounces white mushrooms, thinly sliced

1 medium yellow onion, halved and thinly sliced

4 large garlic cloves, thinly sliced

1 cup Marsala wine (or dry sherry)

3 tablespoons unsalted butter, sliced

Juice from 1 large lemon

COOK THE CHICKEN: Season the chicken breasts on both sides with salt. In a large skillet set over medium heat, heat 3 tablespoons of the olive oil until it smokes lightly. Use a pair of metal tongs to arrange the chicken cutlets in a single layer in the pan and cook on their first sides until browned, 5 to 8 minutes. Turn the cutlets onto their second sides and cook for an additional 3 to 5 minutes, until cooked through and no longer opaque. Remove the chicken and arrange on a serving platter to rest while you build the sauce.

MAKE THE SAUCE AND SERVE: In the same pan over medium heat, heat the remaining 1 tablespoon olive oil. Add the mushrooms, onion, garlic, and a pinch of salt and cook, stirring occasionally, until the mushrooms are tender and the water cooked out, 3 to 5 minutes. Add the Marsala and reduce until almost all of the liquid has cooked down. Whisk in the butter and lemon juice and taste for seasoning. Drizzle the sauce over the cutlets and serve.

CLASSIC CHICKEN PARMESAN

SERVES 4 TO 6

This is a dish pretty much anyone wants to eat all the time, so your job as a cook is to make this the way we all imagine the flavor in our heads. I believe the secret to a great chicken parm is to make the sauce, chicken, and cheeses individually delicious and *then* combine. The thoughtfulness in every part will reward you with an exceptional version of an iconic dish. It's critical to develop extraordinary flavor in the tomato sauce—it needs to be punchy and addictive. Like the bun that covers a burger, the sauce coats the chicken, so it's always the first thing we taste along with the cheese. My dad's tomato sauce has a lot of tomato horsepower, so I use his recipe and layer it with the chicken, basil, mozzarella, and Parmesan. Don't get imaginative with cheeses or herbs here. We Italian Americans like what we like.

CHICKEN

3 large eggs

2 cups panko breadcrumbs

¼ cup finely grated Parmesan cheese

1 pound or 4 (4-ounce) boneless, skinless chicken breasts, sliced horizontally ¼ inch thick, and then pounded even thinner

Kosher salt

2 tablespoons extra-virgin olive oil

2 tablespoons unsalted butter

ASSEMBLY

Dad's Triple-Tomato Marinara (page 113)

Leaves from 6 sprigs fresh basil

2 cups shredded whole-milk mozzarella cheese

1 cup finely grated Parmesan cheese

BREAD THE CHICKEN: Crack and whisk the eggs with a splash of cold water. In another medium bowl, combine the breadcrumbs and cheese. Season the chicken pieces on both sides with salt and dip each thoroughly in the eggs and then in breadcrumbs to coat. Place the chicken in a single layer on a baking sheet. Refrigerate for at least 1 hour, or up to 4 hours.

COOK THE CHICKEN: Preheat the oven to 375°F. Line a baking sheet with paper towels. Heat the olive oil and butter in a large skillet set over medium heat until the butter begins to froth. Add the chicken pieces in a single layer and raise the heat to medium-high (cook in batches if needed). Cook until golden brown, 5 to 8 minutes. Use a slotted metal spatula to gently turn them onto their second sides and cook for an additional 3 to 5 minutes, until cooked through and no longer opaque. Transfer to the paper towel–lined plate and season with salt.

ASSEMBLE: Remove the excess grease from the pan. Add the tomato sauce and cook over medium heat until it soaks up the breadcrumbs and grease from cooking the chicken and is warmed through, 2 to 3 minutes. Remove from the heat. Layer half of the chicken in a single layer in a 10-inch baking dish. Top with half of the sauce, all of the basil, and about half of the mozzarella and Parmesan. Top with the remaining chicken, sauce, and cheeses.

BAKE: Place in the oven and bake until hot and bubbling, 25 to 30 minutes. Switch the oven to broil and broil until golden brown and bubbling on top, 2 to 3 minutes. Serve family style, of course.

PS: I think a piping hot meal is underrated. A lot of what can make food tasty and comforting is extreme heat—so do serve this straight from the oven.

CHICKEN THIGHS PIZZAIOLA

SERVES 6 TO 8

This is a carnivore's cornucopia, and when I know I'm going to make it, I think about eating it all day long. Spicy, browned sausage parked against the tasty chicken thighs with tomatoes and onions as the connectors? Sign me up. (It also tastes so good the next day that sometimes I'll cook up a pot and purposefully leave it in the fridge for dinner the following night.) You could use sweet sausage if you don't like spice, but spicy pork sausage enhances the sauce and takes the chicken to the next level. You can also use chicken breasts if you want it to be a little less rich but just as hearty. The sauce really insulates the chicken and keeps it juicy even when it's cooked through. Serve it up with some spaghetti and go to town.

4 spicy Italian pork sausages (about 1 pound total)

1 cup dry white wine

2 tablespoons extra-virgin olive oil

6 bone-in chicken thighs (about 2 pounds total)

Kosher salt

2 medium yellow onions, halved and thinly sliced

4 large garlic cloves, thinly sliced

1 (28-ounce) can peeled whole tomatoes

1 pint cherry tomatoes, stemmed

1 tablespoon red wine vinegar

Loaf of crusty bread or cooked spaghetti, for serving

COOK THE SAUSAGES: Heat a large cast-iron or stainless-steel skillet over high heat. When the skillet is hot, use a pair of metal tongs to arrange the sausages in a single layer. Reduce the heat to medium and brown the sausages on all sides until cooked through, 8 to 10 minutes total. Transfer the sausages to a medium bowl. Pour off the grease from the skillet, add the wine, and simmer over medium heat to reduce to about ¼ cup liquid, 2 to 3 minutes. Pour the reduced wine over the sausages.

COOK THE CHICKEN: Wipe the skillet clean, set over high heat, and add the olive oil. Season the chicken on all sides with salt. When the oil begins to smoke lightly, add the thighs in a single layer and brown on the first sides, 5 to 8 minutes. Use metal tongs to turn the thighs to their second sides and brown for an additional 3 to 5 minutes. Transfer the chicken to the bowl with the sausages, leaving the grease in the pan.

MAKE THE SAUCE: In the same skillet, combine the onions, garlic, and ½ cup water and cook over medium-low heat, stirring from time to time with a wooden spoon, until the onions are translucent, 8 to 10 minutes. Stir in the canned tomatoes, cherry tomatoes, and 1 cup water and simmer gently until the sauce is somewhat thick and tasty, 20 to 25 minutes.

FINISH: Stir the sausages and chicken (and any meat juices that have collected in the bowl) into the sauce and raise the heat to medium. Bring to a simmer, stir in the red wine vinegar, and shut off the heat. Let it rest for 10 minutes before serving with a loaf of crusty bread or cooked spaghetti on the side.

ROASTED CHICKEN DIAVOLO

SERVES 4 TO 6

The inspiration for spicy chicken started with my daughter, Ava. We often go to Eataly, the Italian market in Manhattan, for this simple roast chicken that's rubbed with Calabrian chile paste . . . it's pretty spectacular. We set out trying to create an even more nuanced spice mix at home and came up with the combination of green, grassy jalapeños and floral Fresno chiles that quickly became our favorite. I like to round it out with a dash of cayenne because dried and fresh chiles link up in a beautiful way. I begin with 1 teaspoon cayenne (which is pretty spicy), but you can add more or less depending on how much you like the heat level. You can also leave some of the seeds in the chiles for added spice. You can roast chicken parts (they'll cook more quickly) or whole as I do below. I marinate for a minimum of 4 hours and up to 12 hours—but no more. The lemons tend to take over too much after that. Serve with a salad, pasta, or roasted vegetables.

½ cup extra-virgin olive oil, plus more for cooking

2 small jalapeño chiles, seeded (for less heat, optional) and coarsely chopped

2 small Fresno chiles, seeded (for less heat, optional) and coarsely chopped

½ teaspoon cayenne pepper

Kosher salt

3 large lemons

1 (3- to 3½-pound) whole chicken

MARINATE THE CHICKEN: Warm the olive oil in a large skillet set over medium heat. Add the jalapeño chiles, Fresno chiles, and cayenne with a pinch of salt. Shut off the heat and let the chiles steep as the oil cools, 25 to 30 minutes. Strain the oil into a large bowl and discard the chiles. Cut two of the lemons into thin rounds and stir them into the oil. Place the chicken in the bowl and rub the marinade all over. Alternatively, place the chicken and marinade in a large, resealable bag and seal. Marinate in the refrigerator for at least 4 hours, or up to 12 hours. I check the chicken while marinating and redistribute the marinade all over to make sure it's coating the meat.

ROAST THE CHICKEN: Preheat the oven to 400°F. Position a rack in the center of the oven. Fit a roasting pan with a rack. Pour the marinade into the pan and set the chicken on the rack, breast side up. Season the chicken with salt. Place the pan in the center of the oven and roast until the juices run clear or a thermometer inserted into the thickest part of the thigh registers 165°F, about 50 to 55 minutes. (I estimate 18 to 20 minutes per pound of bird, so for a 3-pound bird I check the juices and temperature after 45 minutes of cooking.)

REST THE CHICKEN: Let the chicken rest in the pan for at least 10 minutes before transferring to a flat surface. Remove the bird from the pan and gently place breast side down on a cutting board so the juices can flow through the breast meat, and rest for an additional 10 to 15 minutes.

FINISH: Turn the chicken breast side up on a cutting board and carve. Taste the meat and season only if needed. Carve the chicken and arrange on a platter or plates. Serve with the remaining lemon, cut in wedges, on the side.

POLLO E PEPERONI

SERVES 4 TO 6

This is a classic Roman dish that you may catch a pleasant whiff of while walking cobblestoned streets at lunchtime either in Rome or NYC's Little Italy. It's almost a hybrid of a chicken cacciatore (page 150) and a sausage and pepper hero sandwich. The chicken and peppers are the driving force, but the salty notes from the pancetta and slight heat from the pepperoni take me to street food in the best way. Make it and let it sit in the fridge until the next day—it will be that much better. Serve with broccolini or with garlic bread (page 231) on the side to sop up the juices.

¼ pound (4 ounces) pancetta, cut into small cubes

3 tablespoons extra-virgin olive oil

4 ounces pepperoni slices

1 (3½- to 4-pound) whole chicken, cut into 8 parts (breasts halved, thighs, and drumsticks; save the wings for another time)

Kosher salt

¼ teaspoon red pepper flakes

1 cup dry white wine

1 (28-ounce) can peeled whole tomatoes

4 large garlic cloves, lightly crushed

3 large red bell peppers

COOK THE PANCETTA: In a large skillet set over medium heat, cook the pancetta in 1 tablespoon of the olive oil, stirring occasionally, until crispy and browned, 3 to 5 minutes. Use a slotted spoon to transfer the pancetta to a small bowl, leaving the fat behind.

COOK THE PEPPERONI: Line a plate with a paper towel. Raise the heat to medium-high under the same skillet, add the pepperoni slices, and cook until browned and almost crispy, 2 to 3 minutes. Drain on the paper towel. Pour off the grease from the skillet and wipe it clean with a paper towel.

COOK THE CHICKEN: Arrange the chicken on a baking sheet in a single layer and season with salt and half the red pepper flakes. Turn the pieces on their other sides and season again with salt and the remaining pepper flakes. Add the remaining 2 tablespoons olive oil to the skillet and return to medium-high heat. When the oil begins to smoke lightly, reduce the heat to medium, and use a pair of metal tongs to carefully add the chicken pieces, skin side down, to the oil. Ignore the temptation to move or turn the pieces. Allow them to deeply brown on their first sides for 5 to 8 minutes. Turn the chicken pieces skin side up and brown for 5 to 8 minutes. Use a spoon to remove excess grease.

BUILD THE SAUCE: Add the wine to the skillet and simmer gently until the liquid all but evaporates, 8 to 10 minutes. Add the tomatoes and garlic and reduce the heat to medium-low. Simmer until the chicken registers 165°F in the thickest part of the meat, 30 to 35 minutes.

CHAR THE PEPPERS: Meanwhile, place the peppers directly on a gas flame and char on all sides until the skin blackens. Refrigerate to allow them to cool, 5 to 10 minutes. Peel and discard skin. (I use a kitchen towel to wipe the skin away.) Cut the peppers open, remove the seeds, and slice the flesh into ½-inch-thick slices.

FINISH: Add the peppers to the sauce and shut the heat off. Let the chicken rest for 10 minutes on the stove. Serve straight from the skillet, topped with the pancetta and pepperoni.

PS: Take these ingredients and add them to your next lasagna or pizza.

TUSCAN-STYLE
FRIED CHICKEN

●

SERVES 4 TO 6

I spoke to my friend Gabriele Bertaccini about Tuscan fried chicken and the surprising additions that make it special: cinnamon and nutmeg. The warm spices we normally associate with apple pies and cinnamon rolls actually meld with the acidity of lemon and take this chicken to another *very* tasty place. Don't overmarinate the chicken because the lemon juice eventually changes the chicken (and not for the better). I could see sneaking this dish onto a red-sauce joint menu and creating quite a stir. I would serve this with a crunchy salad or some roasted vegetables on the side.

MARINADE

Juice from 2 large lemons

3 large garlic cloves, grated

Kosher salt

2 teaspoons freshly ground black pepper

2 teaspoons garlic powder

½ teaspoon ground cinnamon

¼ teaspoon ground nutmeg

1 (3- to 3½-pound) whole chicken, cut into 10 pieces (breasts halved, wings, thighs, and drumsticks)

FRYING

1½ quarts canola oil, for frying

1 cup all-purpose flour

1 cup cornstarch

3 large eggs

Kosher salt

2 sprigs fresh rosemary

4 sprigs fresh thyme

1 large lemon, cut into wedges

MAKE THE MARINADE: In a large bowl, whisk together the lemon juice and garlic with a generous pinch of salt. Stir in the black pepper, garlic powder, cinnamon, and nutmeg. Mix the chicken pieces in the marinade, tossing to coat. Press the chicken down in a single layer and cover with plastic. Refrigerate for at least 1½ hours, or up to 4 hours.

recipe continues →

CHICKEN & POULTRY DISHES

TUSCAN-STYLE FRIED CHICKEN *continued*

GET READY: Preheat the oven to 350°F.

Pour the oil into a deep, heavy-bottomed pot and heat to 350°F over medium heat. Prepare two baking sheets, one fitted with a kitchen towel and another with a rack.

COAT THE CHICKEN: In a large bowl, combine the flour and cornstarch. In a medium bowl, lightly beat the eggs with a splash of cool water. Remove the chicken from the marinade and discard any excess liquid. Season the chicken with salt and toss in the flour mixture. Shake off the excess, then dip each, one at a time, in the eggs, dredge through the flour, and place on a plate or baking sheet. Separate the larger pieces from the smaller ones.

FRY THE HERBS: When the oil is hot, drop one sprig of rosemary into the oil to test. It should rise to the surface of the oil and crisp in 1 to 2 minutes. Remove with the slotted spoon to the towel-lined baking sheet. Fry the remaining rosemary in the same way and then the sprigs of thyme. Season with salt.

FRY THE CHICKEN: Drop half of the larger pieces of chicken into the oil and gently swirl the oil as they fry. This swirling will assure they fry more evenly on all sides. When they are light to medium brown, 5 to 7 minutes, remove them with the spoon and lay them out on the rack in the baking sheet. Season with salt and transfer to the oven. Make sure the oil returns to the correct temperature and cook the rest of the chicken in batches, keeping the cooked chicken warm on the baking sheet in the oven until all are cooked. When finished frying, leave the chicken in the oven for at least 10 minutes to insure all are cooked through.

SERVE: Arrange the chicken on a serving platter. Stem the rosemary over the chicken so the needles fall right on the meat. Do the same with the thyme. Serve with lemon wedges on the side.

ITALIAN AMERICAN FOREVER
• 168 •

CORNISH HENS
WITH LENTILS

SERVES 4

It's surprising the way the earthy lentils in this simple dish bring out the rich flavors of crisped poultry skin, and it is so special. The sweetness of the honey and the bracingly acidic notes of the vinegar remind me of an agrodolce dish. Cornish hens often get mistaken for the larger Guinea hen, but they're not as gamey. They are like mini chickens and can be a welcome addition to the table with a pasta dish or salad. They do have a pleasantly hearty texture and flavor and are a nice change from chicken.

LENTILS

1 pound green lentils, rinsed

1 tablespoon extra-virgin olive oil

2 dried bay leaves

2 tablespoons unsalted butter

1 tablespoon red wine vinegar

Kosher salt and freshly cracked black pepper

CORNISH HENS

2 tablespoons extra-virgin olive oil

2 Cornish hens (about 1¼ pounds each), halved down the middle

24 to 30 small pearl onions

3 tablespoons honey

3 tablespoons red wine vinegar

Preheat the oven to 350°F. Position a rack in the center of the oven.

COOK THE LENTILS: In a large pot, combine the lentils, olive oil, and bay leaves with 4 cups water. Bring to a simmer and reduce the heat to low. Simmer the lentils, uncovered, until they are tender, 25 to 30 minutes. (*Note:* If you need to add more water for the lentils to finish cooking, add a little at a time. There will be more flavor in the lentils if you cook them and end up with very little liquid at the end of the process. The flavor will be in the lentils instead of down the drain with the discarded cooking liquid!)

COOK THE CORNISH HENS: Line a baking sheet with parchment paper. In a large skillet set over medium heat, heat the olive oil. When the oil begins to smoke lightly, remove the pan from the heat and add the Cornish hen halves, in a single layer, skin-side down. Return the pan to medium heat and brown for 5 to 8 minutes. Turn the hens onto their second sides and brown for 2 to 3 minutes. Transfer the hens to the baking sheet and set the skillet aside. Bake the hens in the center of the oven for 20 to 25 minutes, until a thermometer registers 165°F in the thickest part of the meat.

MAKE THE SAUCE: Meanwhile, pour off and discard the excess grease from the hens' skillet, return to medium heat, and add the pearl onions. Season with salt and cook, stirring from time to time with a wooden spoon, until translucent and tender, 15 to 18 minutes. Add the honey and cook until it froths and browns, 3 to 4 minutes more. Remove the pan from the heat and carefully add the vinegar. Return the pan to medium heat and cook until the sauce thickens and becomes glossy, about 2 to 3 minutes. It should smell like honey and vinegar at the same time. Remove from the heat.

FINISH THE HENS: Remove the hens from the oven and toss them right in the pan with the sauce. Arrange on the serving platter and top with the onions and the sauce.

FINISH THE LENTILS: Warm the lentils over low heat and swirl in the butter and vinegar. Season with salt and pepper and discard the bay leaves. Transfer the lentils to a bowl and serve alongside the Cornish hens.

Like a Sunday sauce or substantial roast, most of these dishes can bubble away all day on the stove or slowly braise in the oven. Osso buco and braciole are two of my favorites because it's nice to have meat dishes where the objective is not a medium-rare interior, but to purposefully overcook the meat low and slow until it falls apart. There are also some more advanced techniques to explore, like stuffed artichokes, if you're feeling adventurous.

CLASSIC

MAINS

BEEF OSSO BUCO page 184

BUONIFICO

Nella proposta gastronomica di Buonifico ti
aspettano piatti della tradizione pugliese e da
tutta Italia. Trovi verdure, cereali e legumi di
vegetale, come tutta una filiera certificata.

BRACIOLE

This dish has many names, including braciole, braciola, involtini, and bruciuluni in Sicilian. No matter the name, the objective is always the same: Add tons of flavor to a tough, lean cut of beef. I cook the filled beef rolls stovetop rather than in the oven because a lot of great, homey cooking happens when you fill the house with the smell of something delicious that bubbles away for hours. Anywhere I see an Italian dish with the addition of aromatic spices, dried fruits, or nuts, I imagine the layered flavors of tart and sweet. This dish gives me Sicilian vibes with the addition of the pine nuts and golden raisins (but if you are not a fan, use dried cherries in their place). The chew from the dried fruit and the creamy richness from the pine nuts give the meat even more flavor and texture, and the acidity of the wine and red wine vinegar brightens the meat, too.

- 12 large garlic cloves, finely chopped
- 1 cup finely grated pecorino cheese, plus more for serving (optional)
- 12 to 14 sprigs curly parsley (stems and all), coarsely chopped
- 2 tablespoons pine nuts
- 2 tablespoons golden raisins
- 2 tablespoons panko breadcrumbs
- 1 teaspoon dried oregano
- Kosher salt and freshly ground black pepper

- 12 thin slices boneless top round of beef (about 2 pounds total)
- 12 thin slices prosciutto
- 2 tablespoons extra-virgin olive oil
- 2 small carrots, cut into ¼-inch-thick rounds
- 2 cups dry red wine
- 2 cups beef stock
- 1 (14-ounce) can peeled whole tomatoes
- 2 tablespoons smooth Dijon mustard
- 1 tablespoon red wine vinegar
- 1 pound cooked orecchiette pasta or polenta, for serving

MAKE THE STUFFING: In a medium bowl, combine a spoonful of the garlic with the cheese, parsley, pine nuts, raisins, breadcrumbs, and oregano. Season with salt and pepper.

MAKE THE ROLLS: Arrange the beef slices in a single layer on a flat surface. Place a prosciutto slice over each piece of beef then sprinkle the filling evenly over the prosciutto. Roll the beef up, tucking in the sides so the filling doesn't fall out as you roll. Close the rolls with toothpicks and place, seam side down, on a baking sheet.

SEAR THE ROLLS: In a large (14-inch) sauté pan with a fitted lid set over medium-high heat, heat the olive oil. When the oil begins to smoke lightly, remove the pan from the heat and add the beef rolls, seam side down, in a single layer. Return the pan to the heat and brown on the first sides, 3 to 5 minutes. Use a pair of metal tongs to turn the braciole a quarter turn, then continue to brown on all four sides, 3 to 5 minutes each. Transfer the rolls to the baking sheet.

BUILD THE COOKING LIQUID: Add the carrots, remaining chopped garlic, and a pinch of salt to the pan. Cook for 1 minute to soften, then add the red wine. Raise the heat to medium-high to bring to a boil, then cook until almost all the wine evaporates, 3 to 5 minutes. Add the beef stock and tomatoes.

COOK THE BEEF: Arrange the beef rolls in a single layer in the pot and reduce the heat to medium. Bring the liquid back to a simmer. Cover and cook over low heat until the beef is tender and easily pierced with a fork, 1½ hours to 2 hours. Whisk the mustard and vinegar into the sauce to thicken.

SERVE: Season with salt and black pepper to taste. Remove the toothpicks and serve the beef and sauce over pasta with additional grated cheese, if desired.

ITALIAN ROAST BEEF

SERVES 8 TO 10

My mother always made roast beef from the top round cut. While it is a pretty lean cut, it's also affordable and the meat has such a great beef flavor. Although there are other options (like a rib roast) that are heartier and offer delicious bones for gnawing, the leanness of the top round also makes it ripe to take on rich flavors and spices. I use roasted garlic to thicken this gravy because it adds richness without being heavy—some of the cloves melt into the gravy while some stay somewhat whole, adding a nice texture. It's also so tasty with the flavor of the beef drippings and the rosemary and oregano that were rubbed all over the meat before roasting. All that's missing are some potatoes (page 212).

MEAT

- 1 (8- to 10-pound) top round beef roast
- Kosher salt
- ¼ cup coarsely ground black pepper
- 2 tablespoons dried oregano
- Leaves from 6 sprigs fresh rosemary
- 3 tablespoons smooth Dijon mustard
- 2 large heads of garlic, halved crosswise
- Extra-virgin olive oil

GRAVY

- 1 cup hearty red wine, such as Chianti or Merlot
- 3 tablespoons grainy Dijon mustard
- 4 cups beef stock
- 1 tablespoon red wine vinegar
- Kosher salt and freshly ground black pepper

Preheat the oven to 500°F. Position a rack in the center of the oven.

PREPARE THE ROAST BEEF AND GARLIC: Fit a roasting pan with a rack. Season the roast beef generously with salt on all sides and arrange on the rack. In a small bowl, combine the pepper, oregano, and rosemary. Spread the mustard directly on the meat and then coat with all of the pepper topping. Arrange the garlic halves on a single layer of foil that is large enough to fold over and cover the garlic. Drizzle with olive oil and season with salt. Wrap the foil over the garlic cloves into a little package. Place in the oven, directly on a rack.

COOK THE BEEF: Place the pan in the center of the oven and cook the beef, undisturbed, for 20 minutes. Lower the temperature of the oven to 350°F and roast for 45 minutes. If the garlic is tender to the touch, remove from the oven and set aside. Continue to cook the beef until a thermometer inserted into the center reads between 130°F and 135°F for medium-rare, about 2 hours longer. When the roast comes out of the oven and rests, the temperature will increase a few degrees as it rests. The end slices will be more well done. If the meat is undercooked, you can always cook it more, but if overcooked, there is no fixing it! Place the roast beef on a cutting board and let rest for 20 minutes.

MAKE THE GRAVY: Pour off the excess grease from the roasting pan. Add the wine to the pan, bring to a boil over medium heat, and reduce the liquid by half. Whisk in the mustard, add the stock, and reduce the heat to low so the sauce simmers until it thickens slightly, 8 to 10 minutes. Add the vinegar and season to taste.

Hold the garlic halves like a half lemon over a blender jar and squeeze the cloves into the blender. Squeeze and reserve a few cloves of garlic to add texture to the gravy. Ladle some of the gravy into the blender and carefully blend until smooth. Whisk the blended garlic back into the gravy. Stir in the reserved cloves for texture. Taste for seasoning.

SERVE: Arrange the beef on a cutting board and look at the natural "lines" of the meat. You want to cut across these lines to tenderize the meat. Cut the roast beef into ¼-inch-thick slices and either serve them from the board with the gravy on the side or transfer the meat to a serving platter.

BISTECCA ALLA FIORENTINA

SERVES 4 TO 6

This steak is an indulgence I normally reserve for ordering in restaurants, but sometimes I want that restaurant meal, the one that transports me to another place. Cooking a 2½-inch-thick porterhouse is an investment and a responsibility. While I generally don't bring meat to room temperature, I leave this meat out on the counter for 30 minutes (because it's quite thick) before cooking. Seasoning the meat properly, searing the steak well, and not overdoing additional flavors are all critical to its success. The garlic powder, combined simply with salt and pepper, creates a thin crust on the meat itself, while the herbs lend vibrancy. I like to cook the steak and let it rest a little before broiling. The heating and resting and reheating of meat tastes more rested (and therefore more delicious) to me. I close my eyes when I take my first bite, and I'm in Tuscany.

1 porterhouse steak, about 2½ pounds and 2½ inches thick

Maldon salt and freshly ground black pepper

1 tablespoon garlic powder

Leaves from 2 sprigs fresh sage

Leaves from 2 sprigs fresh rosemary

Remove the steak from the refrigerator and place on a plate. Let sit out at room temperature for 30 minutes, then preheat the broiler.

MAKE THE RUB: In a small bowl, combine 1 tablespoon salt with 2 teaspoons pepper and the garlic powder. Rub it all over the steak.

COOK THE STEAK: Heat a cast-iron skillet large enough to hold the steak over high heat until it begins to visibly smoke. Use a kitchen towel to "blot" any excess moisture from both sides of the steak. Remove the skillet from the heat and use a pair of tongs to place the steak squarely in the pan. Return to high heat and brown the steak on the first full side, 3 to 5 minutes. Resist the temptation to move it as it cooks. Reduce the heat to medium and cook for an additional 8 to 10 minutes. Raise the heat back to high, turn the steak onto its second full side, and brown for 3 to 5 minutes. Reduce the heat to medium-low and cook on the second side for 8 to 10 additional minutes. Turn the steak on the edge with the fat "cap" and brown that for 3 to 5 minutes. Reduce the heat to low, lay the steak flat, and cook for an additional 3 to 5 minutes on each side.

TEST FOR DONENESS: The simplest way to check a steak for doneness is to make a small incision by the center bone in the thickest part of the steak and check the meat itself. Ideally, the steak should be a little less cooked than you would like to allow for carry-over cooking. For rare, a 2½-inch-thick porterhouse steak will take 35 to 40 minutes to cook. Add a few extra minutes for medium-rare. If using a meat thermometer, rare registers between 125 and 130°F; medium-rare, 130 to 135°F; and medium, 135 to 140°F.

recipe continues →

BISTECCA ALLA FIORENTINA *continued*

FINISH: Remove the steak from the pan and set aside on a baking sheet to rest for 10 minutes. In the same pan set over medium heat, fry the sage and rosemary until they are crispy, 2 to 3 minutes. Transfer the herbs to a paper towel–lined plate and set aside. Run the steak under the broiler for about 2 minutes, until browned and sizzling on top. Transfer to a cutting board and begin by cutting down the length of the larger cut of meat (the strip steak) close to the bone, leaving no meat behind. Cut the strip crosswise (against the grain) into ½-inch-thick slices. Put the slices concisely back together and put them closer to the bone. Do the same with the smaller cut of meat (the filet). This way, the meat will be sliced for easy eating, but the steak will retain its shape. Top the steak with the rosemary and sage and serve.

PORK LOIN BRAISED IN MILK

SERVES 4

It's surprising how the sweetness and acidity of milk make pork loin extra juicy, rich, and tender. We don't think of milk as being acidic or sweet, but in this recipe it plays both of these parts. You definitely want to use a heavy-bottomed pan here because you are cooking the meat all the way through on top of the stove instead of transferring it to the oven. Cooking on the stovetop allows you to control the heat so the pork loin can braise nice and slowly. As the milk and cream tenderize the pork, the acidity from the milk creates a deliciously (and surprisingly) light and vibrant sauce.

2 tablespoons extra-virgin olive oil

1 (1½-pound) center-cut pork loin

Kosher salt and freshly ground black pepper

Leaves from 2 sprigs fresh sage

1½ cups whole milk

1 cup heavy cream

1 large lemon

6 sprigs fresh flat-leaf parsley (stems and all), coarsely chopped

SEAR THE PORK LOIN: Heat a Dutch oven over medium-high heat and add the olive oil. Season the pork loin on all sides with salt and pepper. When the oil begins to smoke lightly, remove the pan from the heat and add the pork loin, skin side down. Return the pan to the heat and brown on the first side, 5 to 8 minutes. Use a pair of metal tongs to rotate the pork a quarter turn to brown a second side, then continue to brown on all four sides, 3 to 5 minutes each. Transfer the meat to a baking sheet to rest.

BUILD THE BRAISE: Pour off the excess grease from the pot. Reduce the heat to low, add the sage, and fry so the flavor mellows slightly, 2 to 3 minutes. Add the milk and cream and raise the heat to medium to bring to a gentle simmer. Peel the lemon as if it were an orange and add the peels to the milk mix, along with the pork.

BRAISE THE PORK: Cover the pot and simmer gently oven medium-low heat, checking from time to time to make sure the cooking liquid looks good. If it gets low, add a little water. Cook until the pork reaches 145°F internal temperature in the thickest part of the meat, 45 to 50 minutes. Remove the meat from the sauce and set it on a cutting board, tented with foil, to rest.

FINISH: Stir the sauce and taste for seasoning. Discard the lemon peels. Slice the pork loin into ½-inch-thick slices and squeeze a little lemon juice directly on the meat. Spoon all of the sauce over the meat and serve sprinkled with the parsley.

PORK CHOPS SCAMPI

SERVES 4

Scampi is an Italian word that loosely translates as "shrimp." That means when we talk about shrimp scampi, we are saying "shrimp shrimp." That said, the scampi sauce we have come to know for shrimp is also tasty with other types of seafood, along with chicken and pork. It's a simple lemon and garlic pan sauce made with the juices given off during searing of the protein as the foundation—in this case, center-cut pork chops rather than shrimp. The breadcrumbs are not necessary, but they add an extra toasty flavor that brings out the deep flavors of the chops.

4 center-cut bone-in pork chops, 1 to 1½ inches thick

Kosher salt

1 tablespoon extra-virgin olive oil

¾ cup dry white wine

3 tablespoons unsalted butter

3 large garlic cloves, grated

½ teaspoon red pepper flakes

½ cup flat-leaf parsley (stems and all), coarsely chopped

Zest and juice from 1 large lemon

1 teaspoon Tabasco sauce

1 teaspoon Worcestershire sauce

½ cup panko breadcrumbs

1 teaspoon dried oregano

COOK THE CHOPS: Season the pork chops on both sides with salt. Heat a large skillet over medium heat and add the olive oil. When the oil begins to smoke lightly, remove the pan from the heat and arrange the pork in a single layer in the skillet. Return the pan to the heat and brown on the first sides, 5 to 8 minutes. Turn the chops onto their second sides and brown for 5 to 8 minutes. Reduce the heat to medium and cook until they reach an internal temperature of 150°F in the thickest part. Transfer the pork to a baking sheet to rest.

MAKE THE SAUCE: Place the same pan over medium heat and add the white wine, 1 tablespoon of the butter, the garlic, the red pepper flakes and a pinch of salt. Simmer, stirring, until the wine all but reduces down and the garlic is tender, 3 to 5 minutes. Arrange the pork chops in the sauce, then warm everything through over low heat. Stir in the parsley, a few grates of lemon zest and the lemon juice, plus the Tabasco and Worcestershire. Taste for seasoning.

TOAST THE BREADCRUMBS: In a medium skillet set over medium heat, melt the remaining 2 tablespoons butter, swirling the pan often, until the white bits in the bottom of the pan turn light brown and the butter smells nutty, 2 to 3 minutes. Stir in the breadcrumbs and toast, stirring, until light brown, then add the oregano.

SERVE: Arrange the pork chops on a serving platter and spoon all the sauce over them. Spoon breadcrumbs over each chop.

LAMB CHOPS SCOTTADITO

SERVES 4

Scottadito is a great Italian word—it's the exclamation of passion referring to something that looks so good that you burn your fingers because you just can't wait to pick it up and eat it! In this case, it's lamb rib chops, which are my favorite lamb chop (though any thick lamb chop you can find will do). To my mind, lamb and anchovies are like Italian "surf and turf," although the anchovies aren't fishy—they simply add umami and balance out the gamey notes of the lamb with their deep, welcome saltiness. Don't like anchovy? Omit it. "Frenched" lamb chops just mean the bones have been cleaned of fat and gristle.

⅓ cup plus 2 to 3 tablespoons extra-virgin olive oil

¼ cup drained capers, coarsely chopped

2 large lemons, zested and halved

5 anchovy fillets, coarsely chopped

5 large garlic cloves, coarsely chopped

18 fresh sage leaves, coarsely chopped

8 (1½-inch-thick) frenched lamb rib chops (about 2 ounces each)

Kosher salt and freshly ground black pepper

2 sprigs fresh rosemary

1 tablespoon honey

MAKE THE MARINADE: In a large bowl, whisk together the ⅓ cup olive oil, the capers, lemon zest, anchovies, garlic, and sage.

MARINATE THE MEAT: Pour half of the marinade on the bottom of a baking sheet and arrange the lamb chops in a single layer on top. Coat the chops with the remaining marinade. Cover with plastic wrap and refrigerate for at least 4 hours, or up to 12 hours. Alternatively, you can marinate the chops in a resealable plastic bag.

GET READY: Remove the lamb from the marinade and season with salt and pepper on both sides.

COOK THE LAMB: Heat a large cast-iron skillet over high heat and add the remaining 2 to 3 tablespoons olive oil. When the oil begins to smoke lightly, add the lamb chops in a single layer. Cook until browned, 2 to 3 minutes, then flip to brown on the second sides, 3 to 5 additional minutes. Turn the chops on their edges and brown the fat on the edges, leaning them against the sides of the pan, 2 to 3 minutes. Add the rosemary and fry with the lamb until crisped and dark green, 2 to 3 minutes. Transfer to a serving platter or wooden board to rest for 10 minutes.

FINISH: Pour any juices from the skillet over the lamb. Heat the skillet again over medium heat and add the lemon halves, cut sides down, and cook until they brown and char slightly, 3 to 5 minutes. Drizzle the lemons with the honey and arrange them alongside the meat. Stem the rosemary right over the meat.

BEEF OSSO BUCO

SERVES 4

Our neighborhood butcher, Rudy Piccinini, used to come to our door and hand off meat directly to my mom. He'd sit in the kitchen sipping coffee and chatting while she cooked. Osso buco means "bone with a hole" and refers to the hole left when the shank or shin bones are cut crosswise and the marrow in the center is exposed. My mom cooked a lot of veal, and veal is what is traditionally used for osso buco, but it's so pricey that I started making it with beef shanks (or shins) instead. I appreciate the roots of this northern Italian classic, topped with a traditional lemon-garlic-parsley combo, aka gremolata, that gives pleasantly bitter and grassy flavors as a counterpoint to the richness of the meat.

OSSO BUCO

¼ cup extra-virgin olive oil

4 (2- to 2½-inch-thick) beef shanks

Kosher salt and freshly ground black pepper

3 medium yellow onions, quartered

3 medium carrots, cut into 2-inch pieces

8 large garlic cloves

2 dried bay leaves

1 cup dry white wine

6 cups beef stock

1 (28-ounce) can peeled whole tomatoes

1 tablespoon Dijon mustard

1 teaspoon red wine vinegar

GREMOLATA

12 sprigs fresh flat-leaf parsley, stemmed and coarsely chopped

2 tablespoons extra-virgin olive oil

2 large garlic cloves, minced

A few grates of lemon zest

Kosher salt

Preheat the oven to 375°F. Position a rack in the center of the oven.

BROWN THE MEAT: In a Dutch oven large enough to hold the shanks in a single layer, heat the oil over medium heat. Season the shanks generously on all sides with salt and pepper. When the oil begins to smoke lightly, add the shanks, cut sides down, in a single layer to the pot. Brown them on the first sides for 5 to 8 minutes. Use a pair of metal tongs to turn to the second sides and brown for just as long. Don't rush the browning; allow the shanks all the time they need. This browning is the most important part of building deep flavor. Remove the meat.

BROWN THE VEGETABLES: Add the onions, carrots, garlic, bay leaves, and then the white wine to the Dutch oven. Simmer over medium heat until the wine is reduced to only a few tablespoons of liquid, 8 to 10 minutes. Return the shanks to the pan and cover with the beef stock, tomatoes, and a little water to submerge the meat, if necessary. Bring the liquid to a simmer and skim any impurities. Cover and place the Dutch oven in the center of the oven. Cook until the shanks are completely tender, 2½ to 3 hours. If the meat is not completely tender, don't be afraid to cook it longer. It's much easier to undercook than overcook this dish.

MAKE THE GREMOLATA: In a small bowl, combine the parsley, olive oil, garlic, and lemon zest with a pinch of salt.

REST THE MEAT: Remove the pot from the oven and let the shanks sit, uncovered, for 15 minutes. Use a large slotted spoon to transfer the shanks to a large serving platter and season with salt. Reduce the liquid in the pot a little over medium heat; whisk in the mustard and simmer until slightly thick. Taste for seasoning. Stir in the vinegar. Remove the bay leaves.

SERVE: Arrange the shanks on individual plates, pour sauce over each, and sprinkle with the gremolata.

ZUCCHINI & EGGPLANT GONDOLAS

SERVES 4

Even though they're so retro, I can't help loving stuffed vegetables. I ate many of them during the years I lived in Europe and the concept just stuck with me. This recipe is a zucchini boat stuffed with a makeshift version of a sweet-sour eggplant caponata, which is made with raisins, vinegar, and pine nuts; all point to Sicily. This can be a main meal on its own for a meatless Monday or a side dish to braised meat or roasted fish. If you don't have a grill, simply roast the eggplant slices alongside the zucchini in a 350°F oven for 25 to 30 minutes instead.

3 tablespoons pine nuts

4 medium zucchini, ends trimmed

Kosher salt

8 tablespoons extra-virgin olive oil

2 large eggplants, cut into ½-inch-thick rounds

2 tablespoons balsamic vinegar

1 large red onion, diced small

4 large garlic cloves, grated

¼ teaspoon red pepper flakes

4 scallions (white and green parts), minced

¼ cup golden raisins

2 tablespoons red wine vinegar

1 tablespoon dried oregano

2 teaspoons sugar

¼ teaspoon ground cinnamon

Leaves from 2 sprigs fresh basil, stemmed

Preheat the grill to medium-high. Preheat the oven to 350°F. Position a rack in the center of the oven. Line a baking sheet with parchment paper.

TOAST THE NUTS: Spread the pine nuts in a thin layer on a baking sheet and toast in the center of the oven until golden brown, 5 to 8 minutes. Remove from the oven and cool.

MAKE THE GONDOLAS: Use a tablespoon measure to scoop the center out of each zucchini, leaving about an inch on each side so it looks like a boat. Set the scooped flesh aside.

ROAST THE ZUCCHINI: Arrange the zucchini gondolas on the lined baking sheet. Season with salt and drizzle with 2 tablespoons of the olive oil. Roast the zucchini until it's tender when pierced with the tip of knife, 18 to 20 minutes. Set aside.

COOK THE EGGPLANT: Drizzle the eggplant slices with 3 tablespoons of the oil and coat both sides, then season liberally with salt. Place the eggplant slices, in a single layer, on the grill. Avoid the very hot spots because charring the eggplant too much can give it an unpleasant flavor. Grill for 5 minutes on the first sides, until slightly yielding and tender. Use a metal spatula or tongs to turn them onto their second sides. Grill until the eggplant is tender, an additional 5 to 8 minutes. Remove from the grill and sprinkle with the balsamic. Cut the slices into a small dice.

FINISH THE FILLING: In a large skillet set over medium-high heat, heat the remaining 3 tablespoons oil. When it begins to smoke, add the onion and garlic and season with salt and the red pepper flakes. Cook, stirring, until they become tender and translucent, 3 to 5 minutes. Stir in the reserved zucchini innards and cook until tender, 3 to 5 minutes. Stir in the cooked eggplant, pine nuts, scallions, raisins, red wine vinegar, oregano, sugar, and cinnamon. Taste for seasoning.

STUFF AND BAKE THE ZUCCHINI: Spoon the hot stuffing into the zucchini gondolas and return them to the oven to bake until hot in the center, 10 to 12 minutes. Remove from the oven and tear the basil leaves and sprinkle on top.

CARMELA SOPRANO'S LASAGNA

SERVES 8 TO 10

If you're a die-hard *Sopranos* fan the way I am, you might remember Junior Soprano's passionate description of Carmela's lasagna to Bobby Bacala. "Sweet sausage . . . layer of basil leaves under the cheese. . . ." I had to recreate it. This meaty lasagna is made tasty by sweet sausages cooked into the sauce and the grassy basil making the most of the mozzarella. I had honestly never leaned into the natural sweetness of tomatoes with ingredients like sweet sausage and basil. I ate my first piece watching *The Sopranos* as an homage. Worth it.

SAUCE

- 4 tablespoons extra-virgin olive oil
- 8 sweet Italian sausages, casings removed
- 2 medium yellow onions, halved and thinly sliced
- 2 medium carrots, thinly sliced
- 6 large garlic cloves, thinly sliced
- Kosher salt
- 1 cup dry white wine
- 1 (28-ounce) can peeled whole tomatoes and their juices
- 1 teaspoon sugar
- ½ teaspoon red pepper flakes

LASAGNA

- Kosher salt
- 1 pound dried lasagna sheets
- 1 tablespoon extra-virgin olive oil
- 2 pounds whole-milk mozzarella cheese, thinly sliced
- 3 cups finely grated Parmesan cheese
- 10 sprigs fresh basil, stemmed

Preheat the oven to 350°F. Position a rack in the center of the oven.

MAKE THE SAUCE: In a large skillet set over high heat, heat the olive oil. Add the loose sausage meat and cook, stirring, so it browns, 5 to 7 minutes. Add the onions, carrots, and garlic and season with a generous pinch of salt. Reduce the heat to medium and cook, stirring from time to time, until the onions become translucent, 5 to 8 minutes. Add the white wine and simmer until almost all of the liquid cooks out, 5 to 8 minutes. Add the tomatoes, sugar, red pepper flakes, and 2 cups water and reduce the heat to low. Simmer until the tomatoes fall apart, 20 to 25 minutes.

COOK THE PASTA: Bring a large pot of water to a rolling boil and add a generous handful of salt. Add the sheets of lasagna and stir with a slotted spoon to make sure they do not clump or stick. Cook for 8 to 10 minutes, until al dente. In a large colander, drain the pasta. Drizzle with 1 tablespoon olive oil. Spread a kitchen towel on a flat surface and spread the sheets out in a single layer so they don't clump or stick.

ASSEMBLE THE LASAGNA: Spoon a little sauce across the bottom of a 9 × 13-inch baking pan, spreading into an even layer. Arrange a layer of one-third of the pasta sheets over the sauce. It's ok if the pasta overlaps. Sprinkle about a quarter of the mozzarella and Parmesan cheese over the pasta and another thin layer of about a quarter of the remaining sauce. Repeat the layering process two more times. For the top layer, add the last of the sauce and then layer the basil leaves on top. Top with the last of the cheese. When you finish, there should be three layers of pasta and four layers of filling.

BAKE THE LASAGNA: Cover the dish tightly with aluminum foil and place on a baking sheet in the center of the oven. Bake for 40 minutes. Raise the temperature of the oven to 450°F and remove the aluminum foil. Bake until the top browns, 8 to 10 minutes. Cool for at least 30 minutes before slicing and serving.

HONEY-BALSAMIC-GLAZED
TUSCAN-STYLE SPARERIBS

SERVES 6 TO 8

I took a lot of inspiration from my weeks in Tuscany filming the Food Network show *Ciao House*, where my cohost, Gabriele Bertaccini (a true Tuscan native), taught me a few things I didn't know about Tuscan food. Take spareribs. For me, pork spareribs were either glazed with soy sauce the way my father made them, or mopped with a classic barbecue sauce the way my mom cooked them up. In Tuscany, however, they're rubbed with a paste made from fennel and rosemary, two ingredients at the heart of Tuscan cooking, and then glazed with honey and balsamic. They're so satisfying to marinate and devour—what a welcome rewrite on a great cut of meat. Look for St. Louis–style ribs; the cartilage and rib tips have been removed, so they cook more uniformly.

RUB

- 2 tablespoons extra-virgin olive oil
- 2 tablespoons fennel seeds
- 2 tablespoons coriander seeds
- 2 tablespoons sesame seeds
- 1 tablespoon sweet paprika
- ½ teaspoon ground allspice
- Leaves from 2 sprigs fresh rosemary, coarsely chopped

(rub continued)

- 2 tablespoons dark brown sugar
- 2 tablespoons smooth Dijon mustard
- 2 tablespoons Worcestershire sauce
- 2 racks St. Louis–style pork ribs (5 to 5½ pounds total)

GLAZE

- ¼ cup honey
- ½ cup balsamic vinegar

MAKE THE RUB: In a medium sauté pan set over low heat, warm the olive oil. Add the fennel seeds, coriander seeds, sesame seeds, paprika, allspice, and rosemary. Gently cook until the spices are just awakened with slight warmth, about 1 minute. Transfer the mix to a medium bowl. Whisk in the brown sugar, mustard, and Worcestershire. Rub the mix all over the racks of ribs. Refrigerate, covered, for at least 6 hours, or up to 12 hours.

COOK THE RIBS: Preheat the oven to 325°F. Position a rack in the center of the oven. Fit a baking sheet with a rack.

Arrange the ribs in a single layer, meaty side up, on the rack in the baking sheet so the ribs are elevated. Cover the whole pan with a layer of foil, seal around the edges, and place in the center of the oven. Bake for 1½ hours. Remove the foil and place the rack back in the oven and bake until nicely browned and tender, 30 to 45 minutes. Remove from the oven and let rest for 10 minutes.

MAKE THE GLAZE: In a medium saucepan set over medium heat, cook the honey until it froths and browns, 3 to 5 minutes. Remove the pan from the heat and carefully whisk in the vinegar. Return the pan to medium heat and cook, whisking occasionally, until the sauce thickens and becomes glossy, about 2 additional minutes. It should smell like honey and vinegar at the same time.

SERVE: Transfer the ribs to a cutting board and stand them upright, holding the end of the bones. Cut down in between each rib and arrange in a single layer on a serving platter. Pour any cooking juices over them and spoon the glaze over top.

STUFFED ARTICHOKES

●

SERVES 6

This is the ultimate Italian American vegetarian main dish. There is no question the noble and meaty artichoke, stuffed with fennel, cheese, and parsley, can go toe to toe with any steak or chicken dinner. These can be assembled entirely in advance and just baked off when needed, and they're so impressive. The fontina, a mild Italian cow's milk cheese, is melty and earthy, while pecorino adds salt and fennel and shallots contribute bright, deep secondary flavors. You can also take a shortcut and use (thawed) frozen whole artichokes—just stuff and bake.

- 6 large artichokes, the very end of the stems trimmed
- 3 large lemons, halved
- 1 cup finely grated Parmesan cheese
- ½ cup extra-virgin olive oil, plus more for drizzling
- ½ cup panko breadcrumbs
- 4 ounces fontina cheese, cubed
- 12 to 14 sprigs fresh curly parsley (stems and all), finely chopped
- 4 large shallots, thinly sliced
- 1 large bulb fennel, tough outer layer removed, quartered and thinly sliced
- Kosher salt
- 2 to 3 tablespoons balsamic vinegar

CLEAN THE ARTICHOKES: Peel off the outer leaves from each artichoke. Prepare a bowl of cold water large enough to hold all the artichoke hearts. Add the juice of 2 lemons and the lemon halves. Use a paring knife to trim the dark green skin from the stem and the base of each artichoke. (Since the stem is edible, why cut it off? Plus, it makes for a more beautiful presentation.) Slice about 2 inches off the top of each artichoke and remove the small (and sharp edged!) inner leaves. Use a tablespoon to scoop out the "hay" or "choke" from the center of each. Squeeze the remaining lemon juice over the artichoke, rub the lemon directly on them (to prevent discoloring), and submerge in the lemon water.

MAKE THE STUFFING: In a large bowl, combine the Parmesan, olive oil, breadcrumbs, fontina, parsley, shallots, and fennel. Season with salt to taste.

Preheat the oven to 350°F. Position a rack in the center of the oven.

STUFF THE ARTICHOKES: Remove the artichokes from the water and pat dry with a kitchen towel. Drizzle a little oil on the bottom of a 9 × 13-inch glass baking dish. Season the artichokes with salt, drizzle with olive oil, and pack the center of each with about 2 hearty tablespoons of the stuffing. The amount of stuffing you need will vary depending on the size of each artichoke. Don't be afraid to really pack the stuffing in the natural crevice of the heart. Arrange the artichokes upright and in a single layer in the baking dish, placing them close together so they steam a little and create moisture as they cook. Top with any remaining stuffing.

BAKE THE ARTICHOKES: Add a little water to the bottom of the baking dish. Cover the dish with a tight layer of aluminum foil, seal the edges, and place in the center of the oven. Bake, undisturbed, for 40 minutes.

FINISH: Remove the dish from the oven. Remove the foil carefully (the steam that gets trapped in there as the artichokes cook can be very hot!) and sprinkle with a little more water. Return the dish to the oven and bake, uncovered, until the artichoke hearts (and not just the stuffing) are tender when pierced with the tip of a knife, 15 to 20 additional minutes. Remove the dish from the oven and allow to cool for a few minutes. I like to drizzle with the balsamic vinegar before serving.

PS: I like to use a tablespoon measure to scoop the silky "hay" out of the artichoke hearts—it scrapes better than a regular spoon.

WHOLE ROASTED FENNEL WITH PARMESAN page 216

SIDE

Side dishes serve many different purposes. A creamy polenta or a potato gratin is the perfect companion to grilled meat or roasted fish. But for other mains, super vinegary cipolline onions or pleasantly bitter broccoli rabe can be just the ticket. The Mini Eggplant Parmigianas are great with Braciole or Lamb Chops Scottadito and can also double as a first course. Explore this chapter for lots of great, simple vegetable ideas, whether as a side dish or even two dishes from this chapter served side by side as a meat-free main. The sleeper hit here? Potato Gratin with Italian "Pizza" Crust—hands down.

DISHES

ROASTED RADICCHIO
WITH ASIAGO CHEESE page 207

POTATO GRATIN WITH
ITALIAN "PIZZA" CRUST
page 212

PORK CHOPS SCAMPI page 180

ROASTED BUTTERNUT SQUASH
WITH AMARETTI COOKIES

SERVES 3 TO 4

Roasted squash and amaretti cookies are a classic southern Italian combination often used as a filling for ravioli. The almond extract in the amaretti cookies is the perfect foil for the fruity notes of the squash and the warm spices. It's very meaty and yet also sweet in the best way—I like to eat it as is, but you can also scoop out the roasted squash and lightly mash it, then sprinkle the cookies over the top. This would be great with Roasted Chicken Diavolo (page 162) or chicken saltimbocca (page 154).

2 or 3 medium butternut or honeynut squash

4 tablespoons (½ stick) unsalted butter

Kosher salt

2 tablespoons dark brown sugar

2 tablespoons blackstrap molasses

½ teaspoon ground cinnamon

¼ teaspoon ground cloves

Zest and juice from 1 large orange

¾ cup lightly crushed amaretti cookies

Preheat the oven to 375°F. Position a rack in the center of the oven. Line a rimmed baking sheet with parchment paper.

GET READY: Place the squash on a flat surface, split each in half lengthwise, and scrape out the seeds. Arrange in a single layer, cut sides up, on the baking sheet.

MAKE THE BROWN BUTTER: In a small saucepan set over medium heat, melt the butter completely, then continue cooking, swirling occasionally, until it starts to turn a light brown color, 3 to 5 minutes. Remove from the heat and immediately distribute the butter evenly among the cavities of the squash halves. Season with salt. Sprinkle the squash halves with the brown sugar, molasses, cinnamon, and cloves. Lightly grate a few zests from the orange. Cut the fruit in half and squeeze all of the juice over and into the cavities of the squash halves.

ASSEMBLE: Fill the bottom of the baking sheet with 1½ cups water to create steam while the squash bakes. Cover the baking sheet with aluminum foil and tightly seal all of the edges.

BAKE THE SQUASH: Place the baking sheet in the center of the oven and bake, undisturbed, for 1½ hours. To check for doneness, pierce one of the halves with the tip of a small knife. The knife should slide in and out easily. If at all firm, bake for an additional 30 to 45 minutes. Remove from the oven. Carefully peel back the foil.

SERVE: Use a metal spatula to transfer the squash halves to a serving platter. Sprinkle with the amaretti cookies and serve.

FRESH CORN "POLENTA" page 205

CLASSIC POLENTA

SERVES 6 TO 8

Corn is the only grain that can also be eaten fresh from the field. Polenta is a close cousin to Southern American grits, and this recipe can employ either. The difference? Grits are generally made from dried white corn (or hominy) while polenta is made from dried yellow corn. The classic way to serve polenta is to load it with butter, milk, cream, and/or cheese, but I like to rely on the sweetness of the corn to act in harmony with cream and sweet mascarpone rather than leaning on the rich saltiness of butter or cheese. Polenta is a wonderful companion to braised or roasted meats or even mushrooms for a hearty vegetarian meal.

1½ cups fine polenta

½ cup heavy cream, at room temperature

8 ounces mascarpone cheese, at room temperature

Kosher salt and freshly ground black pepper

2 to 3 teaspoons sugar

COOK THE POLENTA: In a large saucepan, bring 3 cups water to a boil. In a medium bowl, whisk the polenta with 2 additional cups water. When the water boils, gradually whisk the polenta–water mix into the boiling water. (Adding the polenta this way helps to prevent lumps.) Cook, stirring every few minutes until the polenta is thickened and tender, 45 minutes to 1 hour. If the polenta feels grainy or sandy, stir in another cup water and cook longer.

SEASON THE POLENTA: When the polenta is cooked and fairly thick, stir in the cream and mascarpone. Adding dairy helps keep the polenta loose and creamy. Season with salt and pepper and add the sugar to taste. Let it rest off heat for 15 minutes before serving. If you like it thicker, cool it longer. (I like mine smooth and even slightly soupy, so I don't let it rest longer than 15 minutes.) If it clumps or firms up too much, heat gently and whisk to smooth it out. Spoon the polenta into a serving bowl and serve family style.

PS: In addition to subbing in grits, you can use the quick-cooking polenta if you want a shortcut.

FRESH CORN "POLENTA"

SERVES 4 TO 6

Polenta (page 204) is such a winter dish to me: It just belongs parked next to slow-cooked beef, pork, or lamb. I wanted a summer equivalent and fresh corn was the perfect recruit. I am channeling canned creamed corn from childhood here. The browned butter and smoky paprika bring out the sweetness of the corn, while the crunch of the corn makes the silky polenta even silkier. This can hold its own with a platter of grilled or roasted vegetables or grilled fish.

10 large ears fresh corn, shucked

4 tablespoons (½ stick) unsalted butter

1 to 2 tablespoons dark brown sugar

¼ teaspoon smoked paprika

Kosher salt and freshly ground black pepper

1 cup heavy cream

PREP THE CORN: Hold one ear of corn upright and, using a serrated knife, slice the kernels off from top to bottom. Don't cut so close that you take pieces of the cob, but cut deep enough to extract the full kernels. Repeat this with six more ears (seven in total). Grate the remaining three ears on a box grater to create smaller pieces, and therefore two different textures.

COOK THE CORN: In a medium saucepan set over medium heat, melt the butter. Continue cooking until it turns light brown, 2 to 3 minutes, swirling occasionally. Remove from the heat and immediately stir in all the corn. Let the corn sit in the butter, off the heat, for 2 to 3 minutes. Season with brown sugar to taste, the paprika, and salt and pepper. Return the pan to medium heat and stir in the cream. Cook, stirring over low heat, until the mixture is cohesive, 3 to 5 minutes. Taste for seasoning and serve.

ROASTED RADICCHIO
WITH ASIAGO CHEESE

SERVES 2 TO 3

When I think about the five or six things I seek out every time I've been lucky enough to be in Italy, bitter leafy vegetables like radicchio are always on the list. Here the radicchio is mixed with a little honey and funky Asiago cheese. These two flavors—the nutty cheese and flowery honey—balance the radicchio's bitterness and the balsamic's natural sweetness perfectly. You could make this with trevisano or endive just as easily. Feel free to use more neutral greens like chopped romaine or Tuscan kale to tone down the bitter notes, if desired. This salad is the perfect wingman next to a steak or a decadent baked pasta.

3 medium heads radicchio, trimmed and quartered lengthwise

½ cup extra-virgin olive oil

Kosher salt

2 tablespoons balsamic vinegar

1 tablespoon honey

¾ cup finely grated Asiago cheese

Preheat the oven to 350°F. Position a rack in the center of the oven.

PREPARE THE RADICCHIO: Arrange the radicchio wedges on a rimmed baking sheet, cut side down, in a single layer. Drizzle the olive oil over them and massage the wedges so the oil has a chance to soak into the layers. Season with salt. Add ½ cup water to the bottom of the baking sheet to create some steam as the radicchio cooks.

BAKE THE RADICCHIO: Place the baking sheet in the center of the oven and roast until the radicchio is tender when pierced with the tip of a knife and all the water has evaporated, 20 to 25 minutes.

SERVE: Arrange the radicchio in a single layer on a serving platter and drizzle with the balsamic and honey. Top with the cheese and serve family style.

CIPOLLINE ONIONS
WITH BALSAMIC

SERVES 4 TO 6

Cipolline onions have a heartiness without being heavy and are so satisfying to cook. When mixed with vinegar and honey, as they are here, they strike a great balance of sweet and sour. Park them next to any chicken dish or the lamb chops on page 183. Sometimes I just put a small bowl of chilled cipollines on my cheese or salumi platter for a more interesting accompaniment than the usual mustard or crudités. You can also add them to an antipasti board with artichoke hearts, olives, and roasted peppers. I had a friend who even snuck them into a homemade martini!

1 tablespoon extra-virgin olive oil

3 pounds medium cipolline onions, peeled

Kosher salt

1 tablespoon honey

½ cup balsamic vinegar

COOK THE ONIONS: Heat a skillet large enough to hold the onions in a single layer over medium heat. Add the oil and onions and season with salt. Brown for 3 to 4 minutes, turn them on their second sides, then add ½ cup water. Continue cooking over medium heat, stirring occasionally, until the onions are almost tender, 12 to 15 minutes.

FINISH: Add the honey and simmer carefully over medium heat until the honey froths and starts to turn a darker shade of brown, 3 to 5 minutes. Be very careful; it gets hot. Shut off the heat and wait for the foam to settle so you can see the color of the honey. Carefully whisk in the vinegar, then return to medium heat and cook to reduce for 5 to 8 minutes, until the vinegar cooks out and the onions are tender when pierced with the tip of a knife. Spoon into a bowl and serve with all of the cooking liquid.

PS: This recipe works for sliced yellow onions or pearl onions as well.

CREAMY, GARLICKY WHITE BEANS
WITH PARMESAN BREADCRUMBS

SERVES 4 TO 6

Most beans are inherently creamy when cooked until tender. In this case, we are adding the ultimate insurance policy: cream itself. You can shortcut this with canned white beans, like cannellini or gigante—just drain the beans of any liquid and rinse them before adding to the garlic cream. If using dried beans, it's important to submerge them in cold water and soak for at least 8 hours (refrigerated) to improve digestibility and make them easier to chew. But if you are really in a pinch and need to save time, you can skip the soaking and drop the beans into boiling water for 2 to 3 minutes, drain, and begin cooking them immediately after. This express blanch method will help soften the texture. Another note: Seasoning beans with salt before they are fully cooked causes them to cook unevenly. Cook them without salt and season at the very end just before serving.

1 cup dried white beans, soaked at least 8 hours and up to 24 hours (refrigerated) and drained; or 1 (15-ounce) can cooked white beans such as cannellini, gigante, or great Northern, drained and rinsed

Kosher salt

10 garlic cloves, peeled

1 cup heavy cream

2 teaspoons Worcestershire sauce

½ cup panko breadcrumbs

½ cup finely grated Parmesan cheese

2 tablespoons extra-virgin olive oil

COOK THE BEANS: In a medium pot, combine the beans with 4 cups water. Bring the water to a simmer and reduce the heat to medium-low. (Do not add any salt yet; beans cook more evenly without salt, so only season them when they are fully cooked.) Simmer the beans, uncovered, until they are fully tender, 45 minutes to 1 hour. Let them sit in the warm water until the garlic cream is ready. (If using canned beans, skip this step.)

BLANCH THE GARLIC: Bring a small pot of water to a boil and add a pinch of salt. Add the garlic cloves and simmer for 1 minute, then drain. Fill the same pot with water, bring to a boil again, and add salt. Add the garlic again, boil for 2 minutes, and drain. Repeat this process one more time. You are blanching the garlic repeatedly to eliminate the bitterness and soften the texture. Drain the garlic and discard any water.

Preheat the oven to 375°F. Position a rack in the center of the oven.

MAKE THE GARLIC CREAM: Return the garlic cloves in the same small pot and add the cream with a pinch of salt. Simmer over medium-low heat, taking care not to boil the cream, until the garlic starts to fall apart, 15 to 20 minutes. Add the Worcestershire sauce. Transfer the mixture to a blender and carefully blend until smooth.

COMBINE: Drain the beans in a colander. Transfer the garlic cream to the beans' pot and warm. Stir in the cooked (or canned) beans. Simmer over medium heat for 3 to 5 minutes, just to warm through. Taste the mix and season with salt to taste. Shut off the heat.

MAKE THE TOPPING AND BAKE THE BEANS: In a small bowl, stir the breadcrumbs with the Parmesan and olive oil. Transfer the beans and cream to a 10-inch ovenproof dish and top with the breadcrumbs. Bake in the center of the oven until the breadcrumbs brown and the mixture bubbles, 10 to 15 minutes. Serve.

BAKED BROCCOLI
WITH GARLIC

SERVES 4

My former mother-in-law bakes broccoli for what seems like the entire day. It's never burned, it's always tasty, and I find the yielding texture extra comforting. Conversely, I grew up with a father who would cook broccoli for 45 seconds and then complain that he had overcooked it. When I was in Rome a couple of years ago, I popped into a trattoria and swore someone stole my mother-in-law's recipe. Turns out it's quite "Italian" to cook broccoli, artichokes, and green beans until they are very tender and almost overcooked by American standards. Peeling the stems makes them more tender and prevents you from having to trim them off and discard. Just a little garlic and lemon is all you need here.

2 heads broccoli (about 1½ pounds each)

¼ cup extra-virgin olive oil

8 large garlic cloves, thinly sliced

Kosher salt

1 large lemon, halved

Preheat the oven to 425°F. Position a rack in the center of the oven.

PREPARE THE BROCCOLI: Place the broccoli on a flat surface. Peel the stems with a vegetable peeler then cut the broccoli in half lengthwise. Cut those halves in half again. In a medium bowl, combine the olive oil and garlic with a generous pinch of salt. Arrange the broccoli in a single layer on a rimmed baking sheet and drizzle with the garlic oil mixture.

BAKE THE BROCCOLI: Place the baking sheet in the oven on the middle rack and, with the oven door open, pour ¼ cup water onto the bottom of the baking sheet. Close the door and bake until the edges of the broccoli brown, 15 to 20 minutes. Insert a small knife into the center part of the stem to check if the broccoli is tender. You want it pretty yielding. If not, bake for 5 to 10 minutes longer.

FINISH: Remove from the oven, squeeze the lemon over the broccoli, and arrange on a serving platter.

POTATO GRATIN
WITH ITALIAN "PIZZA" CRUST

SERVES 10 TO 12

One of my favorite potato food groups is the humble gratin, a simple celebration of potatoes and cream. And in the case of this recipe, mozzarella and Parmesan, too. Then I thought about all of the seasonings I add to pizza at a local slice joint and felt like they'd be dreamy on top of a potato gratin. When this emerges from the oven, it smells like a combo of French fries and pizza, only homemade. Serve with roasted vegetables or next to a Bistecca alla Fiorentina (page 177).

GRATIN

1 tablespoon unsalted butter, at room temperature

8 large garlic cloves, minced

7 or 8 medium Idaho baking potatoes (2 to 3 pounds total), peeled and cut into ⅛-inch-thick slices

Kosher salt and freshly ground black pepper

2 cups heavy cream

3 cups whole milk

¼ teaspoon ground nutmeg

½ cup finely grated Parmesan cheese

1½ cups shredded mozzarella cheese (not fresh mozzarella)

CRUST

1 cup panko breadcrumbs

½ cup finely grated pecorino cheese

4 tablespoons (½ stick) unsalted butter, at room temperature

2 tablespoons extra-virgin olive oil

2 tablespoons garlic powder

2 tablespoons onion powder

1 tablespoon dried oregano

½ teaspoon red pepper flakes

GET READY: Preheat the oven to 400°F. Position a rack in the center of the oven. Grease the bottom and sides of a rectangular 12-inch-long gratin dish with the butter. Sprinkle a little of the minced garlic on the bottom of the dish.

COOK THE POTATOES: Place the potato slices in a large saucepan, season liberally with salt and pepper, and mix to blend. Cover with the cream, milk, remaining garlic, and the nutmeg and stir to combine. Simmer gently over low heat for 10 minutes, or until the potatoes are just tender. Take care not to stir the mixture too frequently so as not to break up the potatoes. Stir in the Parmesan cheese. Taste for seasoning.

ASSEMBLE: Arrange half of the potatoes in the dish. Layer in half of the mozzarella cheese and season with salt, then cover with all of the remaining potatoes. Season with salt again and top with the remaining mozzarella cheese. Place the gratin dish in the center of the oven on a baking sheet (to catch any spillage). Bake until the potatoes are tender when pierced with the tip of a small knife, about 1 hour. Remove from the oven.

MAKE THE TOPPING AND BAKE: In a medium bowl, combine the breadcrumbs, pecorino, butter, olive oil, garlic powder, onion powder, oregano, and red pepper flakes. Spread and sprinkle the topping over the potatoes. Return the dish to the oven and bake until the topping is light brown, about 15 minutes. Cut into wedges and serve.

FRIED ZUCCHINI

SERVES 4 TO 6

This is a classic Italian American dish that just never gets old. It requires some advance planning, but then it's fry and devour time. You can also fry some additional herbs (basil or parsley) and some paper-thin lemon slices to make this like a vegetarian fritto misto. The combination of the salty Parm in the breading with the zucchini and then the hit from the lemon are what make this dish. I like to pull out the Campari or Aperol and make some Negronis or spritzes while frying (and eating).

1½ cups panko breadcrumbs

½ cup finely grated Parmesan cheese

4 large eggs

4 medium zucchini, trimmed and cut into ¼-inch rounds

Kosher salt

4 cups canola or avocado oil

6 sprigs fresh oregano

Lemon wedges, for serving

PREPARE THE BREADING: In a medium bowl, combine the breadcrumbs and Parmesan cheese. In another medium bowl, whisk the eggs with 1 tablespoon cool water.

BREAD THE ZUCCHINI: In a large bowl, toss the zucchini rounds with salt. Working a few at a time, dip the zucchini rounds in the egg and then turn in the breadcrumbs until they are coated on all sides. Arrange the breaded slices in a single layer on a baking sheet. Refrigerate for at least 30 minutes, or up to 12 hours.

GET READY: Pour the oil into a deep, heavy-bottomed pot with a fitted lid and thermometer and heat to 350°F. Test the oil by dropping in one piece of zucchini: It should rise to the surface fairly quickly, bubble, and fry. Line two baking sheets with kitchen towels and have a slotted spoon ready.

FRY THE OREGANO: Drop the oregano in the oil and fry until it turns a darker green color, 1 to 2 minutes. Remove with the slotted spoon and spread on one of the towel-lined baking sheets. Season with salt.

FRY THE ZUCCHINI: Drop about one-third of the breaded zucchini into the oil and gently, slowly swirl the oil with a slotted spoon so they fry evenly. When they are light to medium brown, 2 to 3 minutes, remove them carefully with the slotted spoon and lay them out on the kitchen towel to cool. Sprinkle with salt. Repeat with the remaining batches of zucchini, bringing the oil back up to temperature before frying more.

SERVE: Arrange the zucchini with the oregano on a large serving platter and serve with lemon wedges on the side.

WHOLE ROASTED FENNEL
WITH PARMESAN

SERVES 2

This dish is directly inspired by chef Nancy Silverton's whole roasted vegetables featured at her Italian restaurant, Mozza, in Los Angeles, where she often serves them right from the oven. So basic, so deeply delicious. To me, this is a great way to make a meaty vegetable for the carnivores in your family, and it gently points to Italian food in the best way. Always buy fennel bulbs that feel heavy (meaning they're juicy inside) and minimally dried out on the exterior. If you see bulbs with the leafy fronds still attached, get those. They are another sign of freshness and that the vegetable has been even more intact. Want to make this dairy-free? Replace the Parmesan coating with panko breadcrumbs or leave the fennel bulbs as is.

2 large bulbs of fennel

¼ cup extra-virgin olive oil

Maldon salt

1 cup finely grated Parmesan cheese

1 large lemon, halved

Preheat the oven to 375°F. Position a rack in the center of the oven. Line a baking sheet with parchment paper.

PREPARE THE FENNEL: Trim and discard the stalks. Trim off the full, tough outer layer of the bulbs and discard. In a large bowl, toss the fennel with the olive oil and season with salt on all sides.

ROAST THE FENNEL: Arrange the fennel bulbs with space between each on the baking sheet. Top with any excess oil from the bowl. Place the baking sheet in the center of the oven and roast for 45 minutes, until the fennel is tender when pierced with the tip of a knife. Remove the baking sheet from the oven, transfer the fennel to the same bowl, and toss with the Parmesan cheese. Arrange again on the baking sheet. Return to the oven and bake until the fennel is completely tender when pierced in the center with a small knife, 10 to 20 additional minutes (depending on how large the bulbs are).

SERVE: Cut into wedges or slices and arrange on a platter. Season again with salt. Squeeze the lemon over the fennel before serving.

PALAZZO BN
Via XXV Luglio 13/A,
73100 Lecce (LE), Italy

ENJOY PALAZZOBN.COM
Reception: +39 0832 408721
Info: booking@palazzobn.ce

MINI EGGPLANT PARMIGIANAS

●

SERVES 8

Usually this is a main course, but it is a real crowd pleaser as a belly-warming vegetarian appetizer. When I make the smaller Parmigianas, I like to go off the beaten path a little bit and use my Vodka Sauce (page 118). I like the bit of cream mixed with the eggplant and cheese.

SAUCE

2 tablespoons extra-virgin olive oil

1 medium yellow onion, finely chopped

2 large garlic cloves, minced

Kosher salt

¼ cup cheapo vodka

2 teaspoons sugar

¼ teaspoon red pepper flakes

1 (14.5-ounce) can peeled whole tomatoes

¼ cup heavy cream, at room temperature

EGGPLANT

5 large eggs

3 tablespoons whole milk

4 cups Italian-style breadcrumbs

1 tablespoon dried oregano

2 medium eggplants (about 2½ pounds total), cut into 24 (about ½-inch-thick) rounds

6 to 8 tablespoons extra-virgin olive oil

Kosher salt

1½ pounds firm mozzarella cheese, cut into 24 thin slices

Leaves from 2 to 3 sprigs fresh basil, plus more for garnish (optional)

1 cup finely grated pecorino cheese

MAKE THE SAUCE: In a medium skillet set over medium heat, heat the olive oil. Add the onion and garlic and season with salt. Stir in the vodka, sugar, and red pepper flakes. Cook the vodka down, stirring from time to time with a wooden spoon, until there is almost no liquid remaining, about 5 minutes. Add the tomatoes, raise the heat to high, and cook, stirring from time to time, until the tomatoes start to fall apart, 15 to 20 minutes.

Taste for seasoning. Stir in the cream. Transfer the sauce to a blender and carefully puree until smooth.

BREAD THE EGGPLANT: In a medium bowl, whisk together the eggs and milk. In another medium bowl, combine the breadcrumbs with the oregano. Dip each slice of eggplant in the egg mixture and then in the breadcrumbs, coating both sides of each slice of eggplant thoroughly. Arrange in single layers on two baking sheets.

Preheat the oven to 425°F. Position a rack in the center of the oven.

COOK THE EGGPLANT: Line a baking sheet with a kitchen towel. In a large skillet set over medium heat, heat 2 tablespoons of the olive oil until it begins to smoke lightly. Use a pair of kitchen tongs to add a single layer of the eggplant to the pan (you'll have to fry them in batches). Cook until golden brown, about 2 minutes on each side. Transfer to the towel-lined baking sheet so the eggplant can drain as the others cook. Season with salt. Repeat with all of the eggplant rounds, adding more oil to the pan as needed.

ASSEMBLE: Put eight 6-ounce ramekins or other ovenproof baking dishes on a baking sheet. Use a spoon to divide about one-quarter of the tomato sauce among all the ramekins. Top each with a slice of eggplant. Top with a mozzarella slice and a few basil leaves. Sprinkle with about one-third of the pecorino. Repeat this layering two more times to make three layers total.

BAKE THE PARMIGIANAS: Transfer the baking sheet with the ramekins to the oven and bake until the cheese is melted and bubbly, 25 to 30 minutes. Serve in the ramekins—take care as they are hot! Top with basil leaves, if using.

BROCCOLI RABE
WITH GARLIC & PEPPERONCINI

SERVES 4

Broccoli rabe, or rapini, is broccoli's bitter, juicy, nose-to-tail cousin with the leaves, buds, and stems all being edible (and delicious). That said, broccoli rabe is technically a closer relative to turnips than broccoli so there are both naturally bitter and sweet flavors working together here. Pepperoncini, which can be made from yellow-green chiles, banana peppers, or yellow wax peppers, are peppers that are pickled in vinegar and sold in jars. They're a great addition because you benefit from the vinegar-soaked peppers and the tasty liquid in the jar. The rabe ends up tasting like the most delicious bite of an Italian deli sandwich, but in vegetable form. Serve this hot or cold.

Kosher salt

3 medium bunches broccoli rabe (about 1½ pounds total)

3 to 4 tablespoons extra-virgin olive oil

¼ teaspoon red pepper flakes

4 large garlic cloves, grated

2 pickled pepperoncini, thinly sliced, plus 1 tablespoon of their brine

½ cup finely grated Parmesan cheese

BLANCH THE RABE: Line a baking sheet with a kitchen towel. Bring a large pot of water to a boil and add a generous pinch of salt. The water should taste like seawater. Add the broccoli rabe and simmer for 1 minute. Use a slotted spoon to remove the rabe and drain on the prepared baking sheet. Pat dry of any excess moisture.

SAUTÉ THE RABE: Heat a 12-inch skillet over medium heat and add the olive oil. When the oil begins to smoke lightly, remove the skillet from the heat and add the broccoli rabe in a single layer. Return the pan to the heat and season with salt and the red pepper flakes. Cook, stirring, until the rabe feels tender when pierced with the tip of a knife, 3 to 5 minutes. Stir in the garlic and toss to coat, 1 minute. Turn off the heat. Stir in the pepperoncini and sprinkle with the brine. Serve sprinkled with Parmesan.

CAULIFLOWER RISOTTO

SERVES 2 TO 4

We are always looking to make lighter versions of the classics and risotto is no exception. Cauliflower is sturdy enough in risotto to take on the creamy notes from cream, pecorino, and Parmesan, but it also stands on its own. To me, cauliflower reminds me of turnips and broccoli; it's got deep root-vegetable notes. It's surprising how sturdy cauliflower, even when cut very small, can be. It truly resembles rice. This would be great with Beef Osso Buco (page 184), which is classically served with a true risotto Milanese, or the saucy Baked Chicken Cacciatore (page 150). You can buy riced cauliflower in the produce section of most grocery stores—or do it yourself by pulsing chopped cauliflower (stems and florets) in a food processor until they are fine and crumbly.

CREAM SAUCE

1 cup heavy cream

½ cup finely grated pecorino cheese

¼ cup finely grated Parmesan cheese

Kosher salt

RICE

2 tablespoons extra-virgin olive oil

2 medium shallots, minced

1 large garlic clove, minced

Kosher salt and finely ground black pepper

2 cups riced cauliflower

Lemon zest

MAKE THE CREAM SAUCE: In a medium pot set over medium heat, warm the cream and slowly stir in the pecorino and Parmesan cheeses. Season with salt. Keep warm.

COOK THE RICE: In a large sauté pan, heat the oil over medium heat. When the oil begins to smoke lightly, remove the pan from the heat and add the shallots and garlic. Season with salt and cook, stirring from time to time with a wooden spoon, until tender and translucent, 3 to 5 minutes. Remove the pan from the heat and sprinkle the riced cauliflower in a thin layer over the bottom. Return the pan to high heat and cook, stirring once or twice, until the cauliflower softens, 1 to 2 minutes.

FINISH: Season with salt, pepper, and a few grates of lemon zest. Stir in the cream sauce and let the risotto rest with the heat off for 3 to 5 minutes to absorb the liquid. The texture should be loose to eat with a spoon but not soupy. If the consistency becomes too firm, stir in 1 to 2 tablespoons hot water to loosen. Serve in a serving bowl or spoon onto individual plates.

The

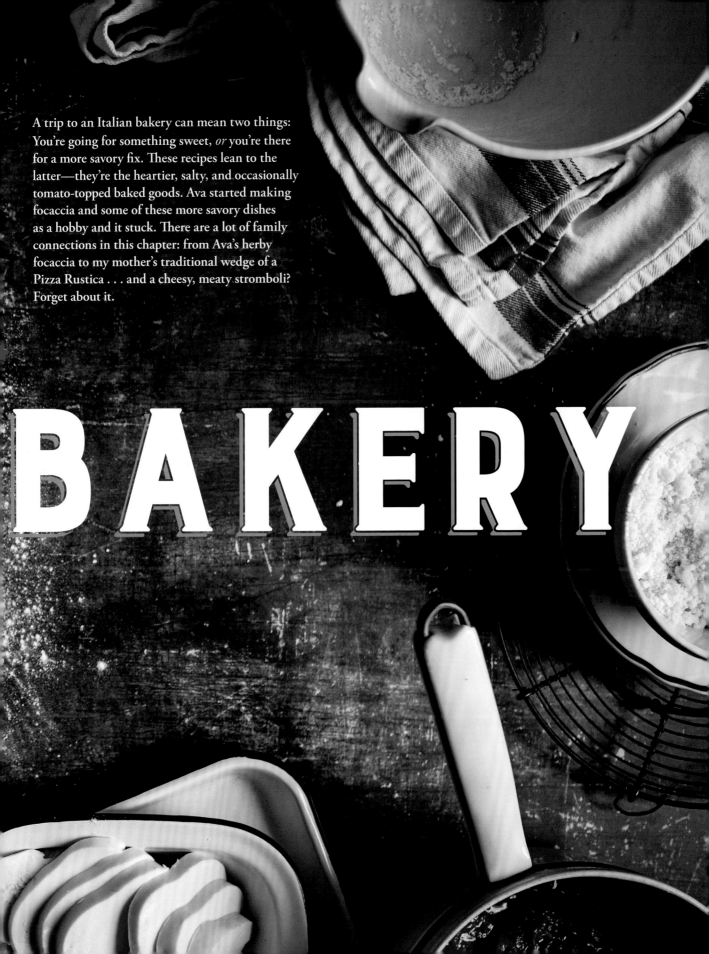

A trip to an Italian bakery can mean two things: You're going for something sweet, *or* you're there for a more savory fix. These recipes lean to the latter—they're the heartier, salty, and occasionally tomato-topped baked goods. Ava started making focaccia and some of these more savory dishes as a hobby and it stuck. There are a lot of family connections in this chapter: from Ava's herby focaccia to my mother's traditional wedge of a Pizza Rustica . . . and a cheesy, meaty stromboli? Forget about it.

BAKERY

AVA'S FOCACCIA

SERVES 10 TO 12

Deliciously yeasty and oily in the best way, focaccia takes well to anything, from a few slices of salami for a sandwich to serving as a side dish to a saucy braised chicken dinner. And it's not uncommon to see squares as part of a breadbasket or served with a cheeseboard. My daughter, Ava, finds comfort in late-night baking and this is one of the best recipes she has developed so far—she'll make the dough before she goes to bed and proof it in the oven until morning and then refrigerate until ready. Thirty minutes after she pops it in the oven, we have fresh focaccia for breakfast—what could be better?

- 3¼ cups all-purpose flour
- 1 tablespoon kosher salt
- ½ teaspoon active dry yeast
- 1 tablespoon sugar
- 1¾ cups warm water (between 100°F and 110°F)
- 4 tablespoons extra-virgin olive oil, plus more as needed
- Leaves from 8 to 10 sprigs fresh thyme
- 2 teaspoons Maldon salt

GET READY: In a large bowl, combine the flour, kosher salt, yeast, and sugar. Add the warm water and mix with your hands until the dough is mixed and sticky. No kneading or mixer required. Pour 2 tablespoons of the olive oil into another large bowl and spread all over the bottom and sides. Transfer the sticky dough to the oiled bowl, turn the dough around in the oil to coat it and cover with plastic, and refrigerate for 2 days.

FORM THE FOCACCIA: Oil a 9 × 13-inch baking dish with the remaining 2 tablespoons olive oil, making sure it is coated evenly. Gently transfer and use your fingers to press the dough into the pan.

PROOF THE DOUGH: Preheat the oven to 150°F (or as low as it will go). Once preheated, shut off the oven and put the dough inside. Let it proof for 5 hours. Remove the dough and preheat the oven to 450°F.

BAKE THE FOCACCIA: Gently press the top of the dough with your fingertips to create "dimples," lightly pressing the dough out until the dough reaches the edges of the dish. (This is called finger docking, and it makes those signature indentations in the focaccia.) Sprinkle evenly with the thyme and Maldon salt. Place the pan in the oven and bake for 12 minutes. Open the oven and rotate the pan halfway. Close the door and bake until golden brown on top, another 12 to 15 minutes. Let it cool for about 5 minutes, then unmold and cool on a wire rack. Transfer to a wood board, cut into squares, and enjoy.

PS: A day or two after it's baked, the oil and thyme soak in more and the flavor intensifies. I like to pop it in the toaster and use it for scrambled egg sandwiches.

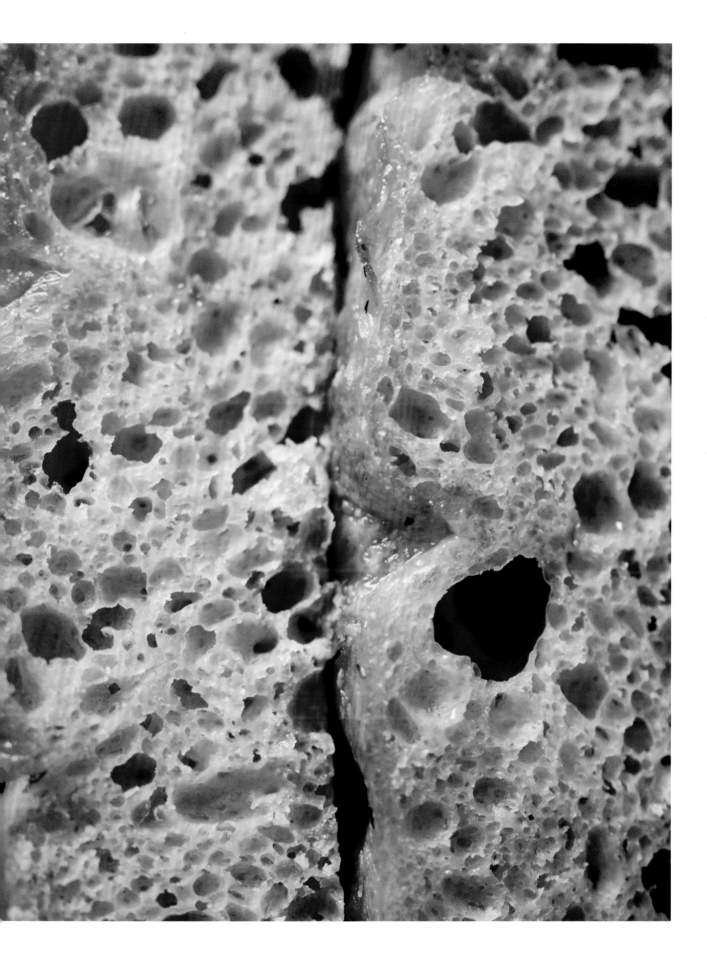

PIZZA RUSTICA

●

SERVES 10 TO 12

Ever have something as a kid and absolutely despise it? Then you revisit it slowly as an adult and fall in love? This recipe has that "where have you been all my life" feeling for me. Pizza rustica isn't a pizza at all—it's a traditional Italian Easter pie. My mom would make it for my dad and we would eat it with fava beans and other symbolically springy things on Easter. My mother's Easter language was all about ingredients and recipes, and this particular one is not for the faint of heart. Imagine a deli sandwich gloriously encased in a quiche-like ricotta pie and here you are. My father would toss up a radicchio or dandelion salad with so much vinegar my lips would swell by the third bite. Such a vivid taste memory. You can either make a traditional round pie with both a top and bottom crust, or make a single crust version in a rectangular dish like in the photo opposite.

DOUGH

3½ cups all-purpose flour, plus extra for rolling

1 teaspoon kosher salt

¼ teaspoon ground nutmeg

¼ teaspoon baking powder

1 cup (2 sticks) unsalted butter, cubed, plus 1 tablespoon for the pan

3 large eggs, lightly beaten

2 tablespoons ice water, plus more as needed

FILLING

1 cup whole-milk ricotta cheese

2 cups diced salami

1 cup diced soppressata

1 cup diced provolone

1 cup diced mozzarella (not fresh)

½ cup finely grated pecorino cheese

½ teaspoon ground nutmeg

Kosher salt and freshly ground black pepper

6 large eggs, lightly beaten, plus 1 large egg for brushing

MAKE THE DOUGH: In the bowl of a food processor, combine the flour, salt, nutmeg, and baking powder. Add the butter and pulse only until just combined and crumbly. Pulse in the eggs and ice water. It should form a smooth ball. If not, pulse in another 1 to 2 tablespoons cold water. Turn the dough onto a flat, lightly floured surface and press into a flat disc. Cover with plastic wrap. Refrigerate for at least 30 minutes, or up to 4 hours.

Preheat the oven to 350°F. Position a rack in the center of the oven. Grease a 9-inch round dish (for a traditional pie) or a 10 × 15-inch baking dish (for a single-crust rectangular pie) with the 1 tablespoon butter.

MAKE THE FILLING: Sprinkle the ricotta all around a large bowl. (Ricotta has already been cooked twice, so overmixing makes the filling tough.) Sprinkle with the salami, soppressata, provolone, mozzarella, pecorino, nutmeg, and some salt and pepper. Stir in the 8 beaten eggs and mix gently to combine until smooth.

ROLL THE DOUGH: Place the dough on the floured surface and divide into two parts: a slightly more generous half of the dough for the bottom crust and the remaining for the top (if making a single-crust pie, don't divide the dough and skip this step and the next step (baking the bottom crust). Using a rolling pin and flour as needed, roll out the larger piece to about a 10-inch circle. Gently place the dough in the pie dish and press onto the bottom and up the sides, leaving a little (between 1 and 2 inches all around) overhang.

BAKE THE BOTTOM CRUST: Cover the dough with a sheet of aluminum foil and some pie weights (or dried beans). Place in the oven and bake until light brown, 13 to 15 minutes. Remove the foil and weights and cool for 15 minutes.

Spread the filling over the bottom crust or, if making the single-crust pie, add the filling to the baking dish.

ROLL THE TOP AND ASSEMBLE: Roll the second portion of dough into about a 10-inch round for the top of the pie (if baking a single crust pie, roll the crust to a sheet slightly larger than the dimensions of your baking dish—you want 1 to 2 inches of overhang). In a small bowl, lightly beat the remaining egg and brush the bottom crust overhang with some of it (reserve the rest). Lay the dough over and seal by pinching the top dough together with the bottom crust (or if making the single crust pie, roll the edges under and crimp or pinch all the way around). Poke holes in the top with the tines of a fork so steam from the filling can escape as the pizza cooks.

BAKE THE PIZZA RUSTICA: Place the dish on a baking sheet and transfer to the center of the oven. Bake for 1 hour until it's golden brown on top and hot in the center when pierced with the tip of a knife. Remove the pizza from the oven cool at least 15 minutes before slicing and serving.

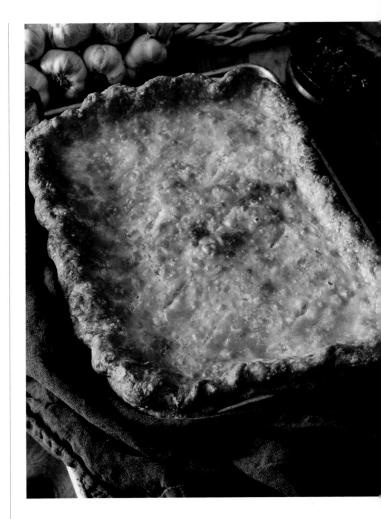

QUADRUPLE GARLIC BREAD

SERVES 4 TO 6

I was a garlic snob for so many years and looked down on garlic powder, even though my father put it in nearly everything he cooked. I figured, why "cheat" and use a dried substitute for the real thing? I thought this until one day, in a pizzeria, I realized I had been systematically dousing my NYC slices with oregano and garlic powder since the beginning of time. Why? Because it tastes incredible. I had a change of heart and never looked back. In fact, I love granulated garlic, the coarser form of dried garlic, just as much as garlic powder. It's chewy and gets stuck in your teeth in the best way. And garlic powder, when used *with* fresh garlic, brings it to a new level. This garlic bread explores multiple iterations of garlic all connecting under one roof. The softer the bread here, the better. Skip the fancy bakery bread, those sentimental childhood loaves studded with sesame seeds from the supermarket are the best.

3 large heads of garlic, halved horizontally, plus 1 head of garlic, cloves peeled and grated

4 tablespoons extra-virgin olive oil

1 tablespoon Maldon salt

1 (13-inch) loaf Italian bread

½ cup (1 stick) unsalted butter, cut into thin slices

2 tablespoons garlic powder

1 tablespoon granulated garlic

2 teaspoons dried oregano

½ teaspoon red pepper flakes

Leaves from 6 sprigs fresh basil

Preheat the oven to 350°F. Position a rack in the center of the oven.

ROAST THE GARLIC: Arrange 3 of the halved garlic heads in a single layer on a sheet of foil large enough to fold over and enclose the garlic. Drizzle with 2 tablespoons of the olive oil and sprinkle with 1 teaspoon of the salt. Cover with the top halves so it looks like the heads of garlic have been reassembled. Wrap the foil around all of the garlic. Bake in the oven until tender when pierced with the tip of a knife, 45 minutes to 1 hour. Carefully open the foil and allow the garlic to cool.

GET READY: Cut the bread in half lengthwise. Arrange the butter slices down the length of the inside and spoon all of the grated garlic and the remaining 2 tablespoons oil on top. Season with the remaining 2 teaspoons salt. Sprinkle with an even layer of the garlic powder, granulated garlic, oregano, and red pepper flakes. Squeeze the garlic from the roasted garlic heads and scatter them all over the bread. Layer the basil leaves along the whole loaf. Close the bread, press down gently, and wrap tightly in foil, folding the ends to seal.

BAKE THE GARLIC BREAD: Put the bread upside down on a baking sheet and bake in the center of the oven until hot to the touch, 25 to 30 minutes. Remove from the oven and turn right side up. Unwrap the bread carefully (as steam will escape), then open up. Return the bread to the baking sheet, cut sides up, and bake for 3 to 5 minutes more so the interior browns slightly.

SERVE: Place the bread on a flat board or bread board, cut into 1-inch slices, and serve.

HOMEMADE PIZZA DOUGH

MAKES 10 TO 12 OUNCES DOUGH (ENOUGH FOR 2 LARGE CALZONES, PAGE 233;
2 STROMBOLIS, PAGE 235; OR 16 GARLIC KNOTS, PAGE 236)

There are options for premade pizza dough in the freezer section of the supermarket and I have even gone to a local pizzeria I like and asked to buy some of their dough. Like store-bought mayonnaise and ketchup, there is no shame in a shortcut that inspires you to try making something new. That said, there is also a pride in making it yourself. Some of the recipes that ask for pizza dough (like the Stromboli, page 235) are more labor intensive, so a shortcut on the dough may inspire you to make it. Some of the other recipes (like Garlic Knots, page 236) are simpler, and that may be a place where you opt to make it from scratch. This is the standard recipe I like to use. Try it!

1½ cups warm water (about 110°F)

2¼ teaspoons active dry yeast

1 tablespoon extra-virgin olive oil, plus more for greasing

3½ cups all-purpose flour, plus extra for rolling

1 scant tablespoon honey

2 teaspoons kosher salt

START THE DOUGH: In a medium bowl, combine the warm water, yeast, and olive oil. Stir to dissolve the yeast, then allow the mixture to rest for 5 minutes, until the mixture looks frothy and cloudy.

ADD THE FLOUR: Using a sieve or fine-mesh strainer, sift about half of the flour over the yeast mixture and blend until smooth with a wooden spoon. Add the honey and salt and mix to blend until smooth. Sift in the remaining flour and mix to blend until smooth.

KNEAD AND PROOF THE DOUGH: Lightly flour a cutting board or flat surface. Turn the pizza dough onto the floured area and knead until the flour feels smooth and the ingredients fully integrated, 3 to 5 minutes. Lightly oil a bowl and place the dough inside. Turn the dough to coat with the oil and cover with plastic wrap. Let it rest in a warm place until it has doubled in volume, about 1½ hours.

Use immediately or wrap in plastic and refrigerate for up to 12 hours.

CLASSIC CHEESE CALZONES

MAKES 2 LARGE CALZONES; SERVES 2 TO 4

A calzone is essentially a pizza folded in half and closed up like a turnover. It's a classic pizzeria dish that I appreciate now more than ever before. The key to a crisp calzone is not to overload the filling with watery ingredients like raw tomatoes. Make your point with a mixture of a few simple flavors, as a filling that's too moist can make the dough soggy. My solution? Load it with cheese! The three cheeses I use are so good when combined: The Parmesan offers a salty flavor; the ricotta contributes a creamy, binding quality; and the mozzarella lends the necessary "cheese pull" factor. And, like a stir-fry, it's also better to have a filling where the ingredients are bite-size so the filling is easy to eat.

- 5 to 6 tablespoons extra-virgin olive oil
- 1 cup whole-milk ricotta cheese, drained of any excess liquid
- 1 cup mozzarella (not fresh), cut into 1-inch cubes
- ½ cup finely grated Parmesan cheese
- 4 sun-dried tomato halves, diced small
- 1 small garlic clove, minced
- 1 teaspoon dried oregano
- 1 teaspoon red pepper flakes
- Kosher salt
- 1 generous tablespoon tomato paste
- All-purpose flour, for rolling
- Homemade Pizza Dough (page 232) or 10 to 12 ounces store-bought
- ½ teaspoon sweet paprika

Preheat the oven to 450°F. Grease two baking sheets with 2 tablespoons of the olive oil.

MAKE THE FILLING: In a large bowl, combine the ricotta, mozzarella, Parmesan, sun-dried tomatoes, garlic, oregano, red pepper flakes, and a generous pinch of salt. Taste for seasoning. Dot the mix with the tomato paste, but don't mix it in. (This way, when you eat the calzone, there will be little bursts of that acidic tomato flavor.)

ASSEMBLE THE CALZONES: Fill a small bowl with water and place it next to your work surface. Lightly flour a flat surface and divide the dough into two equal portions. Use a rolling pin to roll the dough into two flat rounds about 10 inches in diameter. Divide the filling between the two rounds, leaving about a ½-inch border all around so the calzones are easy to fold and seal. Fold each dough round over the filling to form a half-moon shape. Seal the edges by dipping your fingers in water and wetting the edge slightly as you press down and fold it closed. Arrange each calzone in the center of a greased baking sheet. Cut three incisions on the top of each calzone so steam can escape while they bake (this helps prevent the filling from seeping out).

BAKE THE CALZONES: Reduce the oven temperature to 425°F and bake until the calzones develop a nice brown color on the outside, 50 to 55 minutes. Mix the remaining 2 to 3 tablespoons olive oil with the paprika and brush the outsides of the calzones after they come out of the oven.

SERVE: Arrange the calzones on individual serving plates. Cut in half, if desired.

SOPPRESSATA & THREE-CHEESE
STROMBOLI

SERVES 8 TO 10

The word "stromboli" comes from a volcanic island off the coast of Sicily, Italy, but this dish is actually the brainchild of a chef from the Philadelphia area. Stromboli can be filled with a variety of meats and cheeses or, alternatively, with any leftover cooked vegetables you may have hanging around your kitchen. I have made it loaded with cooked eggplant, roasted tomatoes, and mozzarella cheese to mimic an eggplant Parmesan turnover; I've also stuffed it with a combination of Bolognese sauce and roasted vegetables—so good. Here I combine a creamy cheese with a melty cheese and a salty cheese and top it off with some spicy salami. Serve hot out of the oven with Mom's Massachusetts Marinara (page 112) for dunking and a salad on the side.

- All-purpose flour, for rolling
- Homemade Pizza Dough (page 232) or 10 to 12 ounces store-bought pizza dough
- 4 tablespoons extra-virgin olive oil
- ½ cup finely grated Parmesan cheese
- 1 tablespoon unsalted butter, at room temperature
- 2 large garlic cloves, grated
- 1¼ cups shredded mozzarella cheese
- Leaves from 6 sprigs fresh basil
- Kosher salt
- 12 thin slices soppressata
- 12 thin slices provolone cheese
- ½ teaspoon sweet paprika Maldon salt

DIVIDE AND REST THE DOUGH: Lightly flour a cutting board or flat surface. Press gently on the dough and turn it onto the floured area. Divide the dough into two equal portions and roll each half into a loose ball. Cover with a clean kitchen towel and allow the dough to rest for 30 minutes.

GET READY: Preheat the oven to 425°F. Position a rack in the center of the oven. Grease the bottom and sides on an 8½ × 13-inch baking sheet with 1 tablespoon of the olive oil and line with parchment.

MIX THE FILLING: In a medium bowl, combine the Parmesan, butter, and garlic and mix into a paste with 1 tablespoon of the olive oil. Stir in the mozzarella and season with kosher salt.

FORM THE STROMBOLIS: Flatten one half of the dough with a rolling pin and gently roll into a rectangle about 10 inches long and 6 inches wide. Layer half of the soppressata and provolone on the dough. Spread half of the mozzarella mix on the dough and top with half of the basil leaves: Imagine you are making a burrito, so you want to leave about 1 inch on three sides and about 2 inches on the bottom free of filling. Top with a layer of half of the soppressata and half the provolone. Fold the two sides in and roll it up like a burrito, with the sides sealed. Slide a large metal spatula underneath and transfer to the prepared baking sheet. Repeat with the second half of the dough and remaining fillings. Cut 3 incisions on the top of each stromboli so steam can escape while they bake (this helps prevent the filling from seeping out).

BAKE THE STROMBOLIS: Place the baking sheet in the center of the oven and bake until golden brown and puffed, 35 to 40 minutes. Transfer to a cutting board and sprinkle with Maldon salt. Let them rest 10 to 15 minutes. Mix the remaining 2 tablespoons of olive oil with the paprika and brush over the top of each stromboli.

SERVE: Use a serrated knife to gently cut each stromboli into 2-inch slices and serve.

GARLIC KNOTS

MAKES 16 KNOTS

Garlic knots are just that: the comfort of that thick knot of bread, the olive oil, the punchy flavor of the garlic, and the pizzeria vibes that follow. Funny how we tend to eat these with pizza made from the same dough . . . I like to dunk them in tomato sauce, pesto, or even salad dressing. They are a great companion to any salad, chicken dish, or even saucy pasta. When left over, I reheat in the oven and slather with some salted butter.

Olive oil, for greasing

All-purpose flour, for rolling

Homemade Pizza Dough (page 232) or 10 to 12 ounces store-bought pizza dough

½ cup (1 stick) unsalted butter, melted

¼ cup finely grated Parmesan cheese

5 garlic cloves, minced

1 teaspoon dried oregano

1 teaspoon garlic powder

Preheat the oven to 400°F. Position a rack in the center of the oven. Lightly grease a baking sheet.

REST THE DOUGH: Lightly flour a cutting board or flat surface. Turn the pizza dough onto the floured area and press gently on the dough. Roll the dough into a 12 × 14-inch rectangle. Cover with a clean kitchen towel and allow the dough to rest for 15 minutes.

FORM THE KNOTS: Using a pizza wheel or large knife, cut the dough lengthwise into eight 1½-inch strips. Cut each strip crosswise into two equal pieces. Gently tie each piece into a loose knot. Arrange in a single layer on the greased baking sheet, about 2 inches apart.

BAKE THE KNOTS: Place the baking sheet in the center of the oven and bake until the knots are golden brown, 18 to 20 minutes.

FINISH: In a medium bowl, combine the melted butter, Parmesan, garlic, oregano, and garlic powder. When the knots come out, toss them directly into the bowl with the garlic mix. Serve hot or at room temperature.

SPUMONI GARDENS-STYLE PIZZA

MAKES 8 TO 10 SQUARE SLICES

This is my homage to a very distinct style of pizza found at L&B Spumoni Gardens in Brooklyn. I grew up in Manhattan and only first tried their pizza a few years ago. I had a traditional square slice followed by an enormous spumoni ice cream (a three-flavor-type that resembles the colors of the Italian flag: cherry, pistachio, and vanilla—or sometimes chocolate). The pizza was the sleeper for me—I had never had one with the cheese underneath the sauce, with pecorino as a salty topping. It was nostalgic and somehow brand new at the same time; I was totally in love. You can take a shortcut and buy the pizza dough or the tomato sauce. The uniqueness is in the assembly and baking.

All-purpose flour, for rolling

Homemade Pizza Dough (page 232) or 10 to 12 ounces store-bought pizza dough

Olive oil, for greasing and brushing

1½ pounds mozzarella cheese, cut into 16 thin slices

Dad's Triple-Tomato Marinara (page 113)

1 cup finely grated pecorino cheese

ROLL AND REST THE DOUGH: Lightly flour a cutting board or flat surface. Turn the pizza dough onto the floured area and press gently on the dough, then roll into a loose ball. Cover with a clean kitchen towel and allow the dough to rest for 30 minutes.

Preheat the oven to 450°F. Position a rack in the center of the oven. Grease the bottom and sides of an 8½ × 11-inch baking sheet with oil and line it with parchment.

Flatten and roll the dough to a rectangle slightly larger than the baking sheet. Transfer the dough to the baking sheet and brush with olive oil to create a barrier that will help to prevent the topping from making the crust soggy.

ASSEMBLE THE PIZZA: Gently prick the dough with the tines of a fork to prevent puffing when the pizza bakes. Arrange the mozzarella in a single layer right on top of the dough. Spoon the sauce over the cheese. Sprinkle liberally with all of the pecorino.

BAKE THE PIZZA: Bake in the center of the oven for 10 minutes. Rotate the pizza halfway and bake for another 10 minutes. Check to make sure the sauce is bubbling and the cheese is browned; if need be, bake for an additional 5 to 8 minutes. Cool for 10 minutes before cutting into 8 to 10 squares and serving.

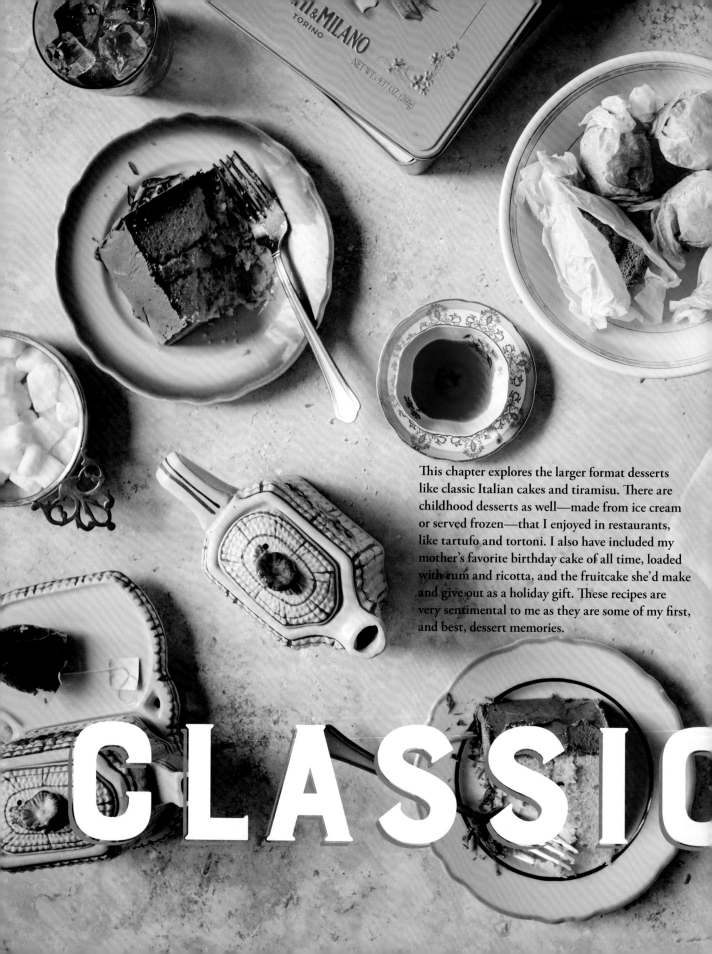

This chapter explores the larger format desserts like classic Italian cakes and tiramisu. There are childhood desserts as well—made from ice cream or served frozen—that I enjoyed in restaurants, like tartufo and tortoni. I also have included my mother's favorite birthday cake of all time, loaded with rum and ricotta, and the fruitcake she'd make and give out as a holiday gift. These recipes are very sentimental to me as they are some of my first, and best, dessert memories.

CLASSIC

CAKES,
Ice Cream & Desserts

MY MOM'S FAVORITE BIRTHDAY CAKE:
CANNOLI-RUM CAKE

SERVES 10 TO 12

My mother always special ordered the cannoli-rum cake from Veniero's bakery in the East Village. It was an off-menu item, so if you didn't know about it, you didn't know about it! There was enough rum in the layers of yellow cake to light it on fire, and the cannoli cream was studded with little chips and lemon zest for taste and texture. She loved the cake so much that she started making it from scratch, and eventually it became her personal birthday cake. Now, when I make one at home, I hold it to the standard of those memories. While I generally have no patience and want to devour dessert as soon as I am finished making it, this cake really benefits from sitting a few hours or even overnight to allow the layers of ricotta cream studded with chocolate chips and lemon zest and pillowy yellow cake to meld together. When it's ready, serve with *hot* coffee or espresso. A note about the filling: If the ricotta has excess liquid inside the container, drain it in a strainer for at least a half an hour before making the filling. Also the outside is lightly frosted with whipped cream that I deliberately leave unsweetened because the other parts of the cake are quite sweet.

CAKE

2 tablespoons plus 1 cup (2 sticks) unsalted butter, at room temperature

2 cups all-purpose flour

2 teaspoons baking powder

1 teaspoon kosher salt

2 cups granulated sugar

6 large eggs

Zest and juice from 1 large lemon

RUM GLAZE

1 cup confectioners' sugar

¼ cup dark rum

FILLING

2 cups ricotta cheese, preferably whole-milk

¾ cup confectioners' sugar

1 teaspoon ground cinnamon

¼ teaspoon ground allspice

1½ cups finely chopped semisweet chocolate (optional)

¼ teaspoon kosher salt

1 large lemon

FROSTING

2½ cups heavy cream

1 (2-ounce) piece/block dark chocolate, for garnish (optional)

Preheat the oven to 350°F. Position a rack in the center of the oven.

GET READY: Grease the bottom and sides of two 9-inch round cake pans with the 2 tablespoons softened butter.

MAKE THE CAKE BATTER: In a medium bowl, combine the flour, baking powder, and salt. In the bowl of an electric mixer fitted with the paddle attachment, cream the remaining 1 cup butter and the granulated sugar on medium speed until smooth, 5 to 8 minutes. Add the eggs one by one, beating until each one is fully incorporated before adding the next. Mix in the lemon zest and juice. Remove the bowl from the machine and use a spatula to stir in the dry ingredients.

BAKE THE CAKE: Fill each cake pan with half of the batter. Bake in the center of the oven until a small knife inserted in the center of each cake emerges clean, 30 to 35 minutes. Wait 15 minutes and then unmold the cakes onto cooling racks. Cool for at least 2 hours, or up to 8 hours.

recipe continues →

CANNOLI-RUM CAKE *continued*

MAKE THE GLAZE: In a medium pot set over medium heat, simmer the confectioners' sugar and rum, whisking until smooth, 3 to 4 minutes. Cool.

MAKE THE FILLING: In a medium bowl, whisk the ricotta until smooth. Sift in the confectioners' sugar, cinnamon, and allspice. Mix to blend. Stir the chocolate chips into the filling if you like.

Lightly zest the lemon over the bowl and stir it into the filling. Set aside.

MAKE THE FROSTING: In a small saucepan, heat 1 cup of the cream over low heat. In a small bowl that fits over the pot with the cream, add the chocolate and salt (make sure the bottom of the bowl doesn't touch the cream). Stir the chocolate occasionally until it is melted. Remove the bowl from the saucepan and transfer the cream to a separate bowl to cool slightly. Fold the warm cream into the warm chocolate, stirring until smooth. Set aside to cool to room temperature.

In a separate bowl (or in the bowl of an electric mixer fitted with the whisk attachment), beat the remaining 1½ cups of cream until stiff peaks form. Using a rubber spatula, gently fold about one-quarter of the whipped cream into the ricotta mixture and reserve the rest.

ASSEMBLE: Place one layer of the cake, flat side up, on a cake stand or serving platter. Brush some of the rum glaze on top and layer with the ricotta filling. Top squarely with the second cake, flat side up, and gently press the two layers together. Spoon the remaining rum glaze over the cake. Using a rubber or metal cake spatula, cover the top and sides of the cake with the ganache frosting. Refrigerate for at least 4 hours before serving. Shave chocolate over the cake by "peeling" thin shavings from the block with a vegetable peeler. Alternatively, use a Microplane grater and grate chocolate over the top.

ORANGE MARMALADE BUNDT CAKE

SERVES 10 TO 12

The flavor of orange or lemon marmalade takes me straight to the Italian coast, where you can always find a juicy slice of blood orange in an Aperol Spritz, or a place like Sorrento, which has enormous lemons that are deliciously sour with super floral zest. Citrus also meanders through various cakes and fruit tarts from around Italy that are always served in the cafés of Rome with the tiniest and strongest espresso. One of my and Ava's favorite spots is Rome's Caffè Greco. When there, we find ourselves sampling the tastiest lemon or orange tart, or a cake flavored with just hints of citrus or jam, like this cake.

FILLING AND GARNISH

2 cups walnut halves, coarsely chopped

1 cup orange marmalade

CAKE

Nonstick cooking spray

1½ cups plus 2 tablespoons (3¼ sticks) unsalted butter, sliced, room temperature

2½ cups sugar

Zest from 1 large lemon

3 cups cake flour

1½ teaspoons baking powder

1 teaspoon kosher salt

6 tablespoons whole milk

4 large eggs plus 2 large egg yolks

2 teaspoons vanilla extract

Whipped cream or ice cream, for serving (optional)

Preheat the oven to 350°F. Position a rack in the center of the oven.

TOAST THE NUTS AND MAKE THE FILLING: Spread the walnuts in a thin layer on a baking sheet and toast in the center of the oven until golden brown, 5 to 8 minutes. Remove the baking sheet from the oven and allow the nuts to cool. In a medium bowl, stir together the marmalade with 1¼ cups of the nuts. Set the filling and remaining nuts aside.

GET READY: Thoroughly grease a 10-cup Bundt pan with cooking spray.

START THE BATTER: In the bowl of a stand mixer fitted with the paddle attachment, beat the butter and sugar on medium speed until fluffy, 8 to 10 minutes. Beat in the lemon zest. Meanwhile, in a medium bowl, combine the flour, baking powder, and salt. In another medium bowl, whisk together the milk, eggs and yolks, and vanilla.

FINISH THE BATTER: With the machine running on low speed, add half of the milk mixture to the butter and blend. Add half of the flour mixture and beat only until just combined. Add the remaining milk and then the remaining flour. Do not overmix.

FILL THE PAN AND BAKE: Spoon about half of the batter into the Bundt pan. Spoon about three-quarters of the walnut marmalade filling in a ring in the middle of the batter. Gently spoon the remaining batter over the filling so it's hidden. Place the pan in the center of the oven and bake until a toothpick inserted in the middle emerges clean, 50 to 55 minutes. Transfer to a wire rack to cool for about 30 minutes.

UNMOLD: Unmold the cake onto a serving platter and top with the remaining marmalade filling and reserved walnuts. Slice and serve with whipped cream or ice cream on the side if you like.

TARTUFO

SERVES 4

The word "tartufo" means truffle, and this crunchy, chocolate-covered ice cream dessert certainly resembles a large, freshly foraged black truffle. But you'll want to crunch through the chocolate coating to get to the chocolate and vanilla ice cream layers inside, with pecans and cherries parked in the center. You can make this with the maraschino cherries, or maybe try with brandy-soaked cherries (amaretto-soaked cherries are great, too) in the center for a boozy note. I also like it more loosely interpreted as a sundae, as it is in the variation, but you can make it either way!

2 cups (1 pint) chocolate ice cream

4 ounces dark chocolate, grated

½ cup pecan halves, coarsely chopped

2 cups (1 pint) vanilla ice cream

12 maraschino cherries, stemmed

2 tablespoons amaretto (or brandy)

¼ cup chocolate sprinkles

4 ounces dark chocolate, melted and cooled

FORM THE CHOCOLATE INTERIOR: Line the insides of four 2-cup bowls with a layer of plastic wrap leaving some overhang on each. Spoon one-fourth of the chocolate ice cream into the bottom of each bowl. Use the back of a spoon to press the ice cream down in the middle so it gets pushed up the sides. Evenly divide half of the grated chocolate and all of the pecans among the four bowls to create a little crunch within. Place the bowls in the freezer for at least 1 hour to allow the ice cream to firm up.

BUILD THE MIDDLES: Remove the bowls from the freezer and spoon a scant quarter of the vanilla ice cream in the center of each. Poke a hole in the center and spoon three cherries and about ½ tablespoon of the amaretto in each. Spoon a little of the remaining vanilla ice cream to cover the cherries. Gather the plastic wrap from the overhang and twist it up to create a ball and pull it out of the bowls. Place the ice cream balls in the freezer to firm up for at least 2 hours, or up to 12 hours.

FINISH: Combine the remaining grated chocolate with the sprinkles on a small plate. Put the melted chocolate in a small bowl. Unwrap the ice cream balls, roll in the melted chocolate, and then in the sprinkle mix. Transfer to a parchment paper–lined baking sheet and freeze for at least 1 hour to set.

SERVE: Place each tartufo on a plate. Cut in quarters for easier eating or leave whole!

FOR TARTUFO SUNDAES: Instead of making the ice cream balls, simply scoop one-fourth of the chocolate ice cream and one-fourth of the vanilla ice cream into each of four bowls. Top with pecans and drizzle with the amaretto. Then top with sprinkles and cherries and serve with melted chocolate on the side for drizzling.

CLASSIC TIRAMISU

SERVES 8 TO 10

I ate so much tiramisu while shooting with the Food Network in Tuscany that I'm going to change the name of the show from *Ciao House* to *Tiramisu House*! Tiramisu loosely translates as "pull/lift me up" in Italian and that's what this iconic dessert has the power to do. My version is classic: rich with silky egg yolks mixed with boozy notes in the filling of cocoa, whipped cream, and mascarpone. The most important steps are making the egg and sugar zabaglione filling (perhaps the hardest one, too, if you know what I mean) and having the patience to let the tiramisu rest 24 hours in the fridge before eating. A zabaglione (sabayon in French) is a fluffy egg-and-sugar mixture that adds richness against the boozy and cocoa flavors—it's so good you can even eat it as a dessert on its own (page 257).

36 to 40 ladyfinger cookies

6 large egg yolks

1 cup sugar

4 tablespoons dry Marsala

1¼ cups heavy cream

1 teaspoon vanilla extract

1½ cups (12 ounces) mascarpone cheese

2½ cups strong brewed coffee, warm

3 tablespoons coffee liqueur

3 tablespoons cocoa powder

4 ounces semisweet chocolate, finely grated

Preheat the oven to 275°F.

GET READY: Arrange the ladyfingers in a single layer on a baking sheet. Place the baking sheet in the oven for 10 minutes to dry them out slightly. Remove and cool.

MAKE THE ZABAGLIONE: Place a roasting pan on a burner on top of the stove and fill about one-third full with warm water. Bring the water to a gentle simmer over medium-low heat. In the bowl of an electric mixer, whisk the yolks with ½ cup of the sugar. Place the bowl in the water bath and hold steady with one hand protected with a kitchen towel or oven mitt. Turn off the heat and whisk the eggs and sugar together steadily until they become fluffy and the eggs are warm to the touch, 4 to 5 minutes. Place the bowl on a stand mixer fitted with the whisk attachment and beat on medium speed until you see traces of the whisk in the eggs and the mix is cooled, 2 to 3 minutes. Mix in 2 tablespoons of the Marsala. Transfer to another bowl and wash the mixer bowl.

MAKE THE MASCARPONE CREAM: In the clean mixer bowl, beat the cream, ¼ cup of the sugar, and the vanilla on medium speed with the whisk attachment until you see traces of the whisk in the cream, 3 to 4 minutes. With the mixer running low, add the mascarpone in spoonfuls until smooth. Whisk into the egg mixture until smooth.

MAKE THE COFFEE MIX: In a medium bowl, combine the coffee with the remaining 2 tablespoons Marsala, the coffee liqueur, and the remaining ¼ cup sugar. Stir until the sugar dissolves.

ASSEMBLE: Using a small fine-mesh strainer, dust the bottom of a rectangular 9 × 13-inch baking dish with 1 tablespoon of the cocoa. Gently drop the ladyfinger cookies, one by one, in the coffee mix and quickly remove (so they don't fall apart). Line the bottom of the dish with about half of the cookies, filling in gaps with half-cookies if needed. Spoon any remaining coffee mix over the ladyfingers. Spoon half of the mascarpone cream over the cookies, covering them evenly. Dust with another tablespoon of the cocoa. Repeat another layer of cookies and then the remaining mascarpone cream on top. Dust with the remaining 1 tablespoon cocoa. Cover and refrigerate at least 24 hours, or up to 3 days.

SERVE: Cut into squares and serve on individual plates. Grate the chocolate on top before serving.

TORTONI

SERVES 8

Until I was twelve, I mistakenly called this classic Italian dessert "torroni," even though it was a dessert I ordered (and ate) time and time again in restaurants. To say this is nostalgic is an understatement. I think it's one of the first dishes that made me recognize the difference between the Italian dishes we made at home and the ones we ate in restaurants. Tortoni originated in a French café, but it was made by an Italian who imported the idea from Italy. It is said that luminaries such as Édouard Manet and Honoré de Balzac enjoyed this sweet dessert, so it should make you feel quite fancy to whip it up and be transported to another time. For me, it takes me back to a time when I was seated in a restaurant, feet not yet touching the floor, as I scooped "torroni" from a bowl.

½ cup sliced almonds

¾ cup sugar

3 large eggs, separated

½ teaspoon cream of tartar

1 teaspoon almond extract

2 cups heavy cream

10 to 12 amaretti cookies

Preheat the oven to 350°F. Position a rack in the center of the oven.

TOAST THE NUTS: Spread the almonds in a thin layer on a baking sheet and toast in the center of the oven until golden brown, 5 to 8 minutes. Set aside and allow to cool.

START THE MERINGUE: In a small pot set over medium-low heat and fitted with a candy thermometer, bring the sugar and ¾ cup of water to a gentle simmer, then continue to cook until it reaches 230°F. In the bowl of a stand mixer fitted with the whisk attachment, whip the egg whites and cream of tartar at high speed until the egg whites hold their shape and the whisk leaves a trace in the whites, 3 to 5 minutes. In a small bowl, whisk the yolks until smooth.

ADD THE YOLKS, SYRUP, AND EXTRACT: Reduce the mixer speed to low, add the yolks to the whites, and beat just until mixed. Slowly stream in the hot syrup so it warms (and cooks) the eggs and forms a glossy mousse, 2 to 3 minutes. Mix in the almond extract and continue beating until the bowl feels cool to the touch, 5 to 6 minutes. Use a rubber spatula to transfer the mixture to a large bowl.

WHIP THE CREAM AND FOLD IN: Wash the stand mixer bowl and the whisk and whip the heavy cream on medium speed until it holds firm peaks. Fold the whipped cream into the egg mixture.

ASSEMBLE THE TORTONI: Arrange eight cupcake liners on a baking sheet that fits in the freezer, then spoon the egg mix to the brim of each liner (or simply spoon all into a large bowl).

MAKE THE TOPPING: In a food processor, pulse the almonds and amaretti cookies until coarsely ground. Spoon the topping liberally over each tortoni. Place the baking sheet in the freezer to firm up the tortoni, at least 3 hours, or up to 48 hours. Serve straight from the freezer, with spoons.

PS: The tortoni can be kept in the freezer for up to 2 days. If freezing more than 12 hours, cover loosely with plastic wrap so they don't absorb other flavors/aromas from the freezer.

ZABAGLIONE

SERVES 4

You have probably seen the French version of this word, sabayon, in restaurants. Sabayon is a more general term for any number of warm, eggy, sweet or savory sauces. Zabaglione, however, is a combination of eggs, sugar, and Marsala. The Marsala is what makes it Italian. It's a wonderfully tasty, fortified wine with earthy, vinegary notes in the most refined and smooth way. I am partial to dry (cheap) Marsala for this, but you can also use sweet Marsala or swap in sherry. All you need to pair it with is plates or bowls of fruit—just spoon the zabaglione right over the top. Note that you need to pay attention when you make this—if you overcook it, it cruelly turns into a sweet omelet of the worst kind. But make it right and it takes you straight to the most perfect meal finale in a fine Italian joint. Try it.

1 generous pint strawberries, hulled and sliced (or raspberries)

⅓ cup sugar, plus more for sprinkling

Juice from ½ large lemon

4 large eggs

¼ cup dry Marsala

GET READY: In a medium pot over medium heat, bring about 2 inches of water to a gentle simmer. Arrange the strawberries in the bottom of four individual bowls. Sprinkle the fruit with a little sugar and the lemon juice and set aside.

MAKE THE ZABAGLIONE: In a medium bowl that fits comfortably over the medium pot, combine the eggs, sugar, and 1 tablespoon water. Put the bowl over the simmering water and cook, whisking steadily, until the egg mix froths, firms, and turns pale yellow, 3 to 5 minutes. If you don't cook the eggs long enough, the zabaglione will become liquidy. If you cook too long, it will turn into scrambled eggs. Take care, and if it seems the mix is getting too hot, remove the bowl from the heat and whisk for a bit. (If it curdles, discard and begin again. This is a delicate balance.)

FINISH: Slowly whisk in the Marsala and continue to cook, while whisking, until the zabaglione doubles in volume and reaches 165°F when a thermometer is inserted in the center of the sauce, 3 to 5 minutes. Spoon all of the sauce over the bowls of fruit, sprinkle with sugar, and serve immediately.

STRAWBERRIES
WITH LIME CURD, BALSAMIC & BLACK PEPPER

SERVES 4

There is nothing that brings strawberries to life like the zest and juice from some good citrus. I use lime here, which is a little more unusual than the more traditional lemon flavor (although I will use a mix and balance of both); I like how it brightens this dessert. That said, I also think vinegar combined with strawberries is genius, and balsamic vinegar has a layered and natural sweetness that lends itself to the dessert category so easily. Then the floral heat from black pepper serves like an alarm clock for this whole dish. You can serve this as is or with crunchy cookies, like biscotti (page 269) or shortbread on the side, or with Ossi dei Morti Cookies (page 274) for crunch and use the lime curd for a great dunk factor. As for the balsamic, if you have a more syrupy, aged one, use it here. A simple one, slightly more liquidy, is great, too—but avoid the cheap stuff for this dessert.

3 large eggs

½ cup sugar

Zest from 1 lemon plus
    ½ cup strained fresh
    lemon juice

Zest and juice from
    2 large limes

2 tablespoons unsalted
    butter, cut into thin
    slices

1 teaspoon kosher salt

1 generous pint
    strawberries, hulled
    and sliced

2 tablespoons balsamic
    vinegar

Freshly ground black
    pepper

PREP THE LIME CURD: In a large, stainless-steel pot, whisk the eggs, sugar, lemon zest, and lime zest until the mixture lightens in color, 2 to 3 minutes. Whisk in the lemon juice and lime juice.

COOK THE LIME CURD: Put the pot over low heat and cook, stirring constantly and taking care to scrape the sides of the pot so the curd doesn't form a crust on the edges or scorch as it cooks, until the mixture starts to thicken, 5 to 8 minutes. Gradually whisk in the butter and salt. Remove the pot from the heat. Transfer the curd to another bowl and cover tightly with a layer of plastic wrap, placing the plastic directly on top of the curd so it won't form a skin as it cools. Cool at room temperature for 45 minutes, then refrigerate for up to 12 hours.

ASSEMBLE AND SERVE: Spoon the curd in the bottom of four individual bowls and layer the strawberries on top. Drizzle with the balsamic. Loosen the grind on your peppermill so it comes out a little coarser than usual, then crack some pepper over the fruit and serve immediately.

PANETONNE BREAD PUDDING

SERVES 10 TO 12

Whenever I get panetonne, the sweet brioche-like bread studded with a variety of nuts, dried fruits, or chocolate, I need to hide some of it away so I can make this bread pudding. (The rest of it? That gets devoured!) It isn't just the flavors and texture of the panetonne, but the yeasty sweetness of the bread itself that marries beautifully with the cream and chocolate the bread pudding filling offers. Try this piping hot with a scoop of ice cream or warm with whipped cream touched with almond extract.

BREAD PUDDING

Nonstick cooking spray

1 pound panetonne

1 cup heavy cream

½ cup granulated sugar

¼ cup packed dark brown sugar, plus more as needed

1 teaspoon kosher salt

½ teaspoon ground cinnamon

1 cup (about 6 ounces) semisweet chocolate chips

2 large eggs plus 1 large egg yolk

2 cups whole milk

1 tablespoon vanilla extract

1 tablespoon almond extract

CARAMEL SAUCE

½ cup granulated sugar

¼ cup heavy cream

2 teaspoons almond extract

1 teaspoon Maldon salt

Ice cream or whipped cream, for serving (optional)

Preheat the oven to 325°F. Position a rack in the center of the oven and place a baking sheet on the rack. Fill it with ½ inch water to create steam as the pudding bakes. Spray the bottom and sides of a 2-quart baking dish with cooking spray.

GET READY: Cut the panetonne into 1½-inch-thick slices and then ½-inch cubes. In a large saucepan over medium heat, whisk together the cream, granulated sugar, brown sugar, kosher salt, and cinnamon and bring to a simmer. Put the chocolate chips in a large, heatproof bowl and pour the warm cream mixture over it. Whisk until smooth. Cool for 5 minutes.

MAKE THE CUSTARD MIX: Whisk the eggs and yolk into the warm chocolate mix. Stir in the milk, vanilla extract, and almond extract. Gently stir in the cubed panetonne, then let it rest and absorb the liquid for 15 minutes.

BAKE THE BREAD PUDDING: Pour the pudding mixture into the prepared baking dish. Place the dish on the baking sheet in the oven and bake until the middle feels firm to the touch, 55 to 60 minutes. Replenish the water in the baking sheet halfway through the cooking. Cool for 15 to 30 minutes.

MAKE THE CARAMEL SAUCE: Place the granulated sugar in a clean medium saucepan and drizzle 2 tablespoons water over it. Swirl the sugar and water together, then bring the mixture to a rolling boil over high heat. Resist the urge to stir with utensils. Reduce the heat to low and cook until the caramel turns golden brown, 3 to 5 minutes. Swirl in the cream, almond extract, and Maldon salt and remove from the heat to cool slightly.

SERVE: Spoon the pudding onto individual serving plates and add ice cream or whipped cream if you like. Pour the sauce over the pudding and serve.

CHRISTMAS FRUITCAKE

SERVES 10 TO 12

My mother made a booze-soaked fruitcake every Christmas when I was growing up. Sometimes she'd make it tinged with lemon, some dried fruit, and almond extract, and it became the Italian hybrid of an American fruitcake from an Italian bakery. It's pleasantly hearty and makes great croutons for ice cream or a budino (pudding) when cubed and toasted. It also makes for dramatic French toast. This lighter, modern fruitcake cake is not so dramatic or booze-soaked and it might just might change your mind about fruitcake. It did for me.

Nonstick cooking spray

2⅓ cups cake flour

¾ cup golden raisins

15 medium dried apricots, diced small

¼ cup candied orange peel

1½ teaspoons baking powder

1 teaspoon kosher salt

½ teaspoon baking soda

½ teaspoon ground cinnamon

½ teaspoon ground nutmeg

½ teaspoon ground cloves

½ teaspoon ground ginger

¾ cup (1½ sticks) unsalted butter, at room temperature

1½ cups granulated sugar

3 large egg yolks

¾ cup plus 2 tablespoons buttermilk

1 teaspoon almond extract

4 large egg whites

¼ teaspoon cream of tartar

GLAZE

½ cup brandy

¾ cup confectioners' sugar

Preheat the oven to 350°F. Position a rack in the center of the oven. Generously spray the bottom and sides of a 9-inch tube pan with cooking spray.

COMBINE THE DRY INGREDIENTS: In a large bowl, combine the cake flour, ½ cup of the raisins, three-quarters of the apricots, the orange peel, baking powder, salt, baking soda, cinnamon, nutmeg, cloves, and ginger.

COMBINE THE WET INGREDIENTS: In the bowl of a stand mixer fitted with the paddle, beat the butter and ¾ cup of the granulated sugar on high until fluffy and pale yellow, 3 to 5 minutes. Reduce to medium speed and add the egg yolks one by one, beating between each before adding the next. Stream in the buttermilk and almond extract and mix just until combined. Gently mix the wet ingredients into the dry ingredients. Do not overmix. Transfer the mix to another bowl and fully wash and dry the mixer bowl.

BEAT THE EGG WHITES: In the bowl of the stand mixer fitted with the whisk, beat the egg whites and cream of tartar at high speed until the egg whites hold their shape and the whisk leaves a trace in the whites, 3 to 5 minutes. Reduce the speed to medium and add the remaining ¾ cup sugar, tablespoon by tablespoon, waiting until each spoonful is incorporated before adding more. Beat for 1 to 2 additional minutes, until the whites are firm and glossy.

FINISH THE BATTER AND BAKE: Fold the cake batter into the egg whites and spoon into the tube pan. Bake in the center of the oven until a small knife inserted in the center emerges clean, 50 to 55 minutes. Cool for 10 to 15 minutes, then unmold onto a serving platter.

MAKE THE GLAZE: In a small pot set over medium heat, simmer the brandy for 5 to 10 minutes to reduce slightly. Sift in the confectioners' sugar, then whisk and simmer until smooth, 2 to 3 minutes more. Stir in the remaining apricots and the remaining ¼ cup raisins. Cool for at least an hour.

SERVE: Spoon the glaze and fruit over the cake. Let it sit for an hour and up to 24 hours (refrigerated) before serving. The longer it soaks, the more pronounced the flavors and texture become. I like it at all stages, honestly. Slice and serve.

RICOTTA CHEESECAKE

SERVES 10 TO 12

The bitter notes of lemon and the rich creaminess of pine nuts are the two flavors that bring this ricotta cheesecake to life. They are such traditional Italian bakery flavors to me. One bite and I close my eyes to find myself standing in front of Ferrara bakery on Grand Street in Little Italy. I am about nine years old and my father is eating a slice of this cheesecake, forkful by forkful, with a searing-hot espresso on the side. The crust is super simple with the tiniest hint of spice—you almost can't even detect it. That's the Italian bakery to me: tiny bursts of flavors adding up to something memorable and delicious.

CRUST

- ½ cup (1 stick) unsalted butter, cubed, plus 1 tablespoon for the pan
- 1½ cups all-purpose flour
- 1 teaspoon kosher salt
- ½ teaspoon ground nutmeg
- 1 large egg yolk, lightly beaten

FILLING

- 1 cup sugar
- 4 large egg yolks
- 2 teaspoons vanilla extract
- 3 cups (about 24 ounces) whole-milk ricotta cheese
- 5 tablespoons pine nuts, toasted
- 2 tablespoons candied citron or candied lemon peels, coarsely chopped
- 1 tablespoon all-purpose flour
- Berries or jam, for serving (optional)

Preheat the oven to 350°F. Position a rack in the center of the oven. Grease the bottom and sides of a 9-inch springform pan with the 1 tablespoon butter. Cover the bottom and sides of the pan with aluminum foil to keep water out as it cooks in the water bath.

MAKE THE CRUST: In a large bowl, combine the flour, salt, and nutmeg. Using your fingers, work the butter into the flour until the mixture resembles coarse crumbs. Gently pat the crust into the bottom of the pan and about 1½ inches up the sides. Brush the egg yolk over the crust to form a protective coating. Cover the crust with a layer of parchment and top with pie weights or dried beans. Place the pan on a wire rack in the center of the oven and bake until the crust is golden brown, 20 to 22 minutes. Remove the pan and leave the oven on. Remove the weights and parchment and cool the crust while you make the filling.

MAKE THE FILLING: In the bowl of a stand mixer fitted with the whisk attachment, beat the sugar, egg yolks, and vanilla on medium speed until pale and lemon-colored, 5 to 8 minutes. Remove the bowl from the mixer and use a rubber spatula to stir in the ricotta, pine nuts, citron, and flour until smooth. Do not overmix.

BAKE THE CHEESECAKE: Smooth the batter over the crust and place the pan on a rimmed baking sheet on a wire rack in the center of the oven. Add about ½ inch of water to the baking sheet to create steam as the cheesecake bakes. Bake for 30 minutes, then lower the oven temperature to 325°F. Bake until a toothpick or small knife inserted in the center emerges clean, 25 to 30 additional minutes. Cool completely on a wire rack and then refrigerate for at least 8 hours or up to 24 hours before serving.

SERVE: Unclasp the sides of the pan to remove the ring. Set the cheesecake, still on its base, on a cake plate. Use a knife (run under warm water, then dry it) to cut into individual slices. Serve as is or with berries or jam on top.

ALMOND FLORENTINE COOKIES page 273

The CARDBO

When I walk into an Italian bakery, I'm usually first greeted by the pastries—the cannolis, babas, and sfogliatella—all the classics that adorn the cases of places like Ferrara bakery on Grand Street in New York City's Little Italy. But as I make my way to the cash register, it's the cookies that catch my eye. They present a visual cornucopia of textures, excesses of almond extract, and an array of chocolate dips and sprinkles in all the right places. This chapter is filled with recipes to make your own box of cookies tied with red string, just like from the bakery.

CHOCOLATE NUT BISCOTTI page 269

OSSI DEI MORTI
page 274

ITALIAN PINCH
COOKIES page 272

ARD BOX

*Tied with the
Red-and-White
String . . .
& Beyond*

PIGNOLI COOKIES page 278

CHOCOLATE NUT BISCOTTI

•

MAKES 24 TO 30

This is chocolate biscotti from all angles; it has pieces of chocolate with cocoa powder and even coffee in the batter to make a deliciously bitter and super chocolatey cookie that rises above most other biscotti, which can often taste dull and stale. Biscotti comes from "bis" meaning twice/two, and "cotti" meaning cooked/baked. Baking, slicing, and then baking a second time give the cookies their simple name. I also find them to be the perfect amount of dessert after a big meal, just a little nibble of something sweet. In Italy, biscotti are often served alongside a sweet wine like vin santo. I like them with piping hot coffee and tea, too.

3 cups all-purpose flour, plus extra for rolling

¼ cup cocoa powder

2½ teaspoons baking powder

1 teaspoon kosher salt

1 cup sugar

½ cup (1 stick) unsalted butter, at room temperature

Zest from 1 small lemon

3 large eggs plus 1 large egg white

1½ tablespoons light corn syrup

1 tablespoon instant coffee

1½ teaspoons vanilla extract

1 teaspoon almond extract

6 ounces semisweet chocolate, coarsely chopped

½ cup walnuts, coarsely chopped

Preheat the oven to 350°F. Line a baking sheet with parchment paper.

MAKE THE DOUGH: In a medium bowl, combine the flour, cocoa, baking powder, and salt. In the bowl of a stand mixer fitted with the paddle attachment, beat the sugar, butter, and lemon zest together on medium speed until combined and slightly fluffy, 3 to 5 minutes. Add the eggs and the egg white, one by one, with the mixer on the same speed, taking care to fully incorporate one before adding another, until fully mixed. Slow the mixer to medium-low speed and blend in the corn syrup, coffee, and the vanilla and almond extracts. Remove the bowl from the mixer and use a rubber spatula to gently stir in the dry ingredients, the chocolate, and walnuts.

FORM AND BAKE THE DOUGH: Transfer the dough to a lightly floured flat surface and use your hands to roll it into a log 10 to 12 inches long. Gently transfer the log to the lined baking sheet. Bake for 35 minutes; the outside should be lightly browned and the dough should feel firm to the touch. Transfer to the flat surface and cool for only 10 minutes.

SLICE THE LOG: With a serrated knife, cut the log into ½-inch-thick slices, using a sawing motion so the cookies don't break. Arrange the biscotti on the baking sheet in a single layer but close together.

BAKE AGAIN: Reduce the oven temperature to 325°F and bake the biscotti until browned, 18 to 20 minutes. Cool. Store in a sealed container for up to 3 days.

PS: Sometimes I don't bake these cookies for a second time and enjoy them somewhat moist and cakey.

ITALIAN BAKERY
CHOCOLATE & JAM
SANDWICH COOKIES opposite   ITALIAN PINCH COOKIES page 272   ALMOND FLORENTINE
COOKIES page 273

ITALIAN BAKERY
CHOCOLATE & JAM SANDWICH COOKIES

MAKES 12 SANDWICH COOKIES

Like rainbow cookies and cannoli, chocolate cookies sandwiched with raspberry or apricot jam are at the heart of any Italian bakery. These are as much about texture as they are flavor—there's nothing like biting down on a crunchy and buttery cookie, having it break in your mouth, and then almost dissolve into a combination of chocolate and tart jam. For these cookies, you'll need a star tip and pastry bag because you want to pipe out the buttery dough to get that bakery look. The rich cookie dough also bakes best when it's cold, so for best results, pipe the batter and freeze for an hour before baking the cookies.

BATTER

1 cup (2 sticks) unsalted butter, at room temperature

¾ cup sugar

1 teaspoon kosher salt

2 large eggs

1 teaspoon almond extract

2¼ cups all-purpose flour

¼ teaspoon baking powder

GLAZE AND FILLING

3 tablespoons heavy cream

8 ounces semisweet chocolate, finely chopped

Rainbow sprinkles

½ cup raspberry jam

MAKE THE BATTER: In the bowl of a stand mixer fitted with the paddle attachment, cream the butter, sugar, and salt on medium speed until fluffy and pale colored, 5 to 8 minutes. With the mixer on low, add the eggs one by one, taking care to fully incorporate the first before adding the second, then mix in the almond extract. Remove the bowl from the mixer and sift the flour and baking powder right over the batter. Use a rubber spatula to fold in the flour until all is just combined. Do not overmix, or your cookies will be tough.

GET READY: Line two baking sheets with parchment. Transfer the batter to a pastry bag fitted with a medium star tip. (Alternatively, cut a corner of a resealable plastic bag, fit with the star tip, and fill with the batter.)

PIPE THE COOKIES: Pipe about 12 cookies in a straight 2-inch line on one baking sheet, leaving at least 1 inch between cookies to allow for spreading when they bake. Repeat with the remaining batter on the second baking sheet. Place both baking sheets in the freezer for 1 hour to chill.

BAKE THE COOKIES: Preheat the oven to 350°F. Place the baking sheets on the center rack of the oven and bake until the cookies are light brown, 12 to 15 minutes. (If they don't fit side by side, bake one sheet at a time.) Cool for at least 30 minutes.

MAKE THE CHOCOLATE GLAZE: In a small saucepan set over medium-low heat, bring the cream to a simmer. Remove from the heat and stir in the chocolate until melted and smooth.

ASSEMBLE: Put the sprinkles on a shallow plate. Dip half of each cookie in chocolate, roll the (concave) top in sprinkles, and put back on the baking sheet so the chocolate can cool, 15 to 20 minutes. Spoon jam down the length of each flat side and sandwich two halves together to make 12 sandwich cookies. Store the cookies in a sealed plastic container for up to 2 days.

PS: Most bakeries favor seedless jam, but I prefer the texture that seeds offer.

ITALIAN PINCH COOKIES

MAKES 36 TO 40 COOKIES

Making these reminds me of forming individual ravioli or tortellini . . . but for dessert. You roll the dough out, cut out rounds, fill them with jam, and then pinch the dough together—hence the name. So many Italian bakery cookies have a jam component, either dotted in the middle or used to sandwich two cookies together—usually it's orange marmalade, apricot preserves, or raspberry jam. These cookies don't spread a lot, so you can arrange them pretty close together on the baking sheet. They also keep, tightly wrapped, for a couple of days, though they likely won't be around that long. Like most Italian cookies, they are designed for coffee sipping in the afternoon. I also have these for breakfast sometimes.

2 cups all-purpose flour, plus extra for rolling

½ cup confectioners' sugar, plus extra for dusting

Zest from 1 large lemon

½ teaspoon baking powder

10 tablespoons (1¼ sticks) unsalted butter, at room temperature

1 teaspoon vanilla extract

2 large eggs

½ cup seedless raspberry jam

COMBINE THE DRY INGREDIENTS: In a large bowl, whisk together the flour, confectioners' sugar, lemon zest, and baking powder.

MAKE THE DOUGH: In the bowl of a stand mixer fitted with the paddle attachment, beat the butter, vanilla, and eggs on high speed until smooth, 2 to 3 minutes. Add the dry mix and beat on low speed until combined and sticky, 4 to 5 minutes. Transfer the dough to a flat surface and roll into a 1-inch-thick disc. Wrap in plastic and refrigerate for 1 hour.

Preheat the oven to 350°F. Line two baking sheets with parchment paper and position a rack in the center of the oven.

ROLL THE DOUGH: Dust a countertop with flour. Use a rolling pin to roll the dough until it is less than ¼ inch thick. Use a 2½-inch round cookie cutter to cut out rounds, wasting as little dough as possible. Gently knead and reroll (and cut) scraps for additional cookies.

FILL AND PINCH THE COOKIES: Place a scant teaspoon of jam in the center of each round. For each round, lift up the opposite sides and pinch the tops together (about three fingertips wide across the top) but leave the ends open. Fold the pinched side down to the left or right side of the cookie. Arrange them on the baking sheets with about 1 inch of space between each.

BAKE THE COOKIES: Place the baking sheets on the center rack and bake until the bottoms are lightly golden brown but the overall cookie is light colored, 12 to 14 minutes. (If the two sheets don't fit side by side, bake one at a time.)

COOL AND DUST THE COOKIES: Transfer the cookies to a wire rack to cool for at least 30 minutes. Dust with confectioners' sugar. Store in a sealed container for up to 3 days.

ALMOND FLORENTINE COOKIES

MAKES 52 TO 60 COOKIES (OR 26 TO 30 LARGER ONES)

While the word "Florentine" references Florence, Italy, these cookies are thought to have originated as French cookies baked in honor of Catherine de' Medici when she came to France. For our purposes, though, let's say they're Italian, and serve them with a favorite bowl of gelato (or better yet, use them to make ice cream sandwiches). Florentines have a crunchy yet delicate almond base and are decorated with a layer of chocolate that is traced with a fork to create a wave pattern and extra ridges. Keep the dough in small balls in the freezer to bake off as needed when you crave a sweet treat.

- 2 cups sliced almonds
- ¾ cup sugar
- 3 tablespoons all-purpose flour
- ½ teaspoon kosher salt
- 5 tablespoons unsalted butter
- 2 tablespoons heavy cream
- 2 tablespoons corn syrup
- ¾ teaspoon vanilla extract
- ½ teaspoon ground allspice
- Nonstick cooking spray
- 8 ounces semisweet chocolate chips

Preheat the oven to 350°F. Position a rack in the center of the oven.

TOAST THE NUTS: Spread the almonds in a thin layer on a baking sheet. Place the baking sheet in the center of the oven and toast the nuts until golden brown, 5 to 8 minutes. Let the nuts cool.

MAKE THE ALMOND MIX: In the bowl of a food processor, pulse half of the almonds a few times until they resemble coarse meal. Pulse in the sugar, flour, and salt until blended. Transfer the mixture to a large bowl and stir in the remaining almonds.

MAKE THE DOUGH: In a medium saucepan set over medium heat, combine the butter, cream, corn syrup, vanilla, and allspice. Bring the mixture to a gentle simmer, stirring to blend with a wooden spoon. Simmer until all of the sugar has dissolved into the cream, 2 to 3 minutes. Set aside to cool.

FORM THE COOKIES: Line a baking sheet with parchment paper and spray with cooking spray for added security. Use a teaspoon measure and spoon 18 to 20 scant teaspoons onto one baking sheet, leaving a few inches space between each. (These cookies spread when they bake; unless you can fit two baking sheets side by side, the cookies are best baked one sheet at a time; for larger cookies use a tablespoon measure to form about 15 cookies on one sheet.)

BAKE THE COOKIES: Bake for 5 or 6 minutes, then rotate the pan halfway. Continue to bake until the cookies are thin and evenly browned, another 5 to 6 minutes. Let cool a few minutes before carefully transferring the cookies with a spatula to an elevated wire rack to cool completely. Repeat with the remaining dough.

MAKE THE CHOCOLATE GLAZE: Place a heatproof bowl over a medium pot with 2 inches of simmering water. Add the chocolate to the bowl and gently melt the chocolate, stirring with a rubber spatula to avoid scorching. Use a pastry brush to brush the flat bottom of each cookie liberally with chocolate, then arrange, chocolate side up, in a single layer on a platter to allow the chocolate to set slightly, about 10 to 15 minutes. Use the tines of a fork to trace a wave pattern in the chocolate (if your kitchen is very warm, refrigerate the cookies for 10 minutes before using the fork to create the wavy lines). Allow the cookies to cool completely. Serve chocolate side up. Store in a sealed container for up to 3 days.

OSSI DEI MORTI COOKIES

MAKES 28 TO 32 COOKIES

Ossi dei morti translates as "bones of the dead" because they are very hard and crunchy (the dough they are made from is almost meringue-like). They are tasty and light on their own, but also make great companions to gelato, sorbet, or pudding. My parents would get them every time they visited the local bakery. I think, for them, ossi dei morti transported them to Sicily (where my mother had some family) and All Souls' Day, where one might commemorate the "bones of the dead" out of respect for lost family members. My memory is of them crunching through the cookies, their shirts covered with sugary dust, the chewy cookie stuck in their teeth, which was always remedied by a sip of hot coffee or espresso to cut through the sweetness and clear out the crumbs. You can also serve the cookies with vin santo (a sweet dessert wine from Tuscany) or grappa.

1 cup unblanched almonds

1½ cups sugar

1 teaspoon baking powder

1 teaspoon kosher salt

2 large eggs

1½ teaspoons fresh lemon juice

¼ teaspoon almond extract

1¼ cups all-purpose flour, plus extra for rolling

Preheat the oven to 300°F. Position a rack in the center of the oven.

TOAST THE NUTS: Spread the almonds in a thin layer on a baking sheet and toast the nuts until golden brown, 5 to 8 minutes. Let the nuts cool completely.

MAKE THE DOUGH: In the bowl of a food processor, pulse the almonds until finely ground. In the bowl of a stand mixer fitted with the whisk attachment, whisk the sugar, baking powder, and salt on medium-low speed. Add the eggs one by one, taking care to fully incorporate the first before adding the second, then add the lemon juice and almond extract with the mixer on the same speed. Add the ground almonds and flour and mix on medium speed until the dough's texture is sticky, 3 to 4 minutes.

Line two baking sheets with parchment paper.

PORTION THE DOUGH: Lightly flour a flat surface. Turn the dough out and form into a ball. Flatten the ball and cut the dough into four equal pieces. Cover three pieces with a kitchen towel while you work with the first piece; the dough dries out quickly unless covered.

FORM THE COOKIES: Roll the dough into a thin rope about ½ inch wide and about 24 inches long. Cut the roll into equal 3-inch pieces with a medium kitchen knife. You should get eight pieces. Arrange the cookies in rows, about 2 inches apart, on one of the prepared baking sheets. Repeat with the remaining three pieces of dough, dividing the cookies between the baking sheets.

BAKE THE COOKIES: Place the baking sheets on the center rack (if they don't fit side by side then place them on the upper-middle and lower-middle racks, switching halfway through) and bake until the cookies are golden brown, 15 to 18 minutes. Remove and cool a few minutes on the baking sheets so the texture firms, then transfer the cookies to a wire rack to cool completely. Store in a sealed container for up to 3 days.

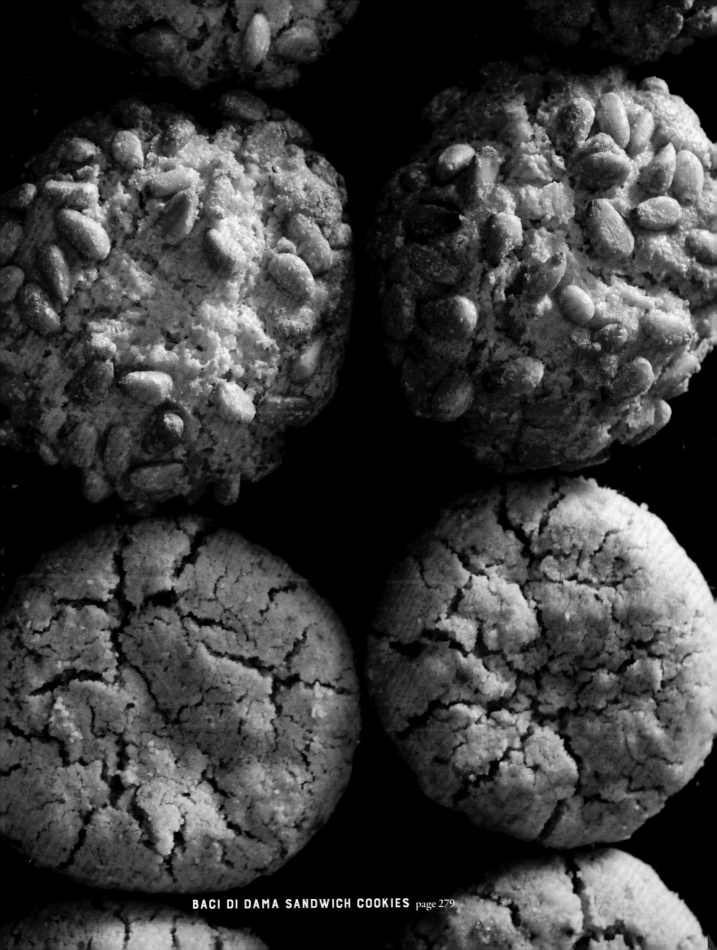

BACI DI DAMA SANDWICH COOKIES page 279

PIGNOLI COOKIES

MAKES 20 TO 22 COOKIES

Pignoli is such a fun word, and my earliest memory of eating delicious pine nuts was biting into this cookie. The burst of almond paste would hit me first, then the creamy, luscious pine nuts would come in as a crunchy backup singer. Wow. To me this is one of the OG Italian bakery cookies. You can sub in sliced almonds in place of the pine nuts if that makes life easier.

2 (8-ounce) cans almond paste

1½ cups granulated sugar

3 large egg whites

1 cup pine nuts

¼ cup confectioners' sugar

Preheat the oven to 350°F. Position one oven rack in the upper-middle position and one rack in the center. Line two baking sheets with parchment paper.

MAKE THE DOUGH: In the bowl of a stand mixer fitted with the whisk attachment, beat the almond paste on high speed until finely crumbled, 3 to 4 minutes. Add the granulated sugar and mix on medium-low speed until fully combined, 2 to 3 minutes. Set the mixer on medium speed and add the egg whites one by one, taking care to fully incorporate one before adding another.

ROLL THE BALLS AND COAT WITH NUTS: Spread the pine nuts in a single layer on a plate. Roll the dough into 20 balls, each about 1 tablespoon. Roll each ball partially in the pine nuts. Flatten the balls slightly, pine nut side up, on the baking sheets with about 1 inch space between each.

BAKE THE COOKIES: Place the baking sheets on the two racks and bake the cookies until browned, 18 to 20 minutes, rotating the pans bottom rack halfway through. Cool for 10 minutes before transferring the cookies to a wire rack to cool completely. Store in a sealed plastic container for up to 3 days.

PS: Read the almond paste package before you buy it to make sure you are not getting marzipan. Almond paste is creamier and less sweet than marzipan (which is stiffer and usually has double the amount of sugar as almond paste).

BACI DI DAMA SANDWICH COOKIES

MAKES 20 TO 22 SANDWICH COOKIES

My mother made these "women's kisses" as part of her holiday cookie basket. They've always reminded me of the flavor of that iconic chocolate-hazelnut spread. I love them while they're still a little warm . . . you know, so they still kind of melt in your mouth? Mom always described these as being a northern Italian cookie—hazelnuts are native to the Piedmont region in the north and this simple cookie was a way to utilize the local crop of nuts. That said, I have seen them in bakeries throughout Italy and you can also find them in bakeries in Manhattan's Little Italy and probably in other Little Italys, too. I love a light bite of chocolate at the end of a meal. With the toasty notes from the hazelnuts, these kisses are an ideal last bite flavor combo.

COOKIES

2 cups blanched (skinned) hazelnuts

1 cup all-purpose flour

⅔ cup sugar

¼ cup cornstarch

1 teaspoon kosher salt

1¼ cups (2½ sticks) unsalted butter, chilled and cubed

2 teaspoons vanilla extract

FILLING

2 tablespoons whole milk

1 cup semisweet chocolate chips

Preheat the oven to 350°F. Position a rack in the center of the oven.

TOAST THE NUTS: Spread the hazelnuts in a thin layer on a baking sheet. Toast in the center of the oven until the nuts are golden brown, 5 to 8 minutes. Let the nuts cool. Turn off the oven.

GET READY: Line two baking sheets with parchment paper. Pulse the hazelnuts in a food processor until they resemble coarse flour.

MAKE THE DOUGH: In a large bowl, whisk together the ground hazelnuts, flour, sugar, cornstarch, and salt. Add the butter and vanilla and work the dough with your fingers until the butter is integrated and the dough is smooth.

FORM THE COOKIES: Roll scant tablespoons of the dough into balls. You'll get 42 to 44 dough balls. Arrange the cookie balls on the prepared baking sheets about 1½ inches apart. Flatten each ball gently. Refrigerate for at least 1 hour, or up to 8 hours.

Preheat the oven to 325°F. Position a rack in the center of the oven.

BAKE THE COOKIES: Place the baking sheets in the center of the oven and bake until the cookies are golden brown, 18 to 20 minutes. (If the baking sheets don't fit side by side, bake one at a time.) Remove from the oven and let cool.

MELT THE CHOCOLATE AND ASSEMBLE: In a medium saucepan set over medium heat, bring the milk to a simmer and shut off the heat. Add the chocolate chips and stir until the chocolate melts and the mixture is smooth.

ASSEMBLE: Place the cookies on a flat surface. Spoon the chocolate on the flat side of one cookie and sandwich with another. Repeat with the rest of the cookies. Store the cookies in a sealed container for up to 3 days.

ACKNOWLEDGMENTS

I always thank my mom and dad despite the fact that they are no longer with me. Even from their resting place in Brooklyn, I can feel them with Ava and me.

Thanks to Aunt Aggie, who taught me what joy is.

Thanks to Aunt Betsy DiBenedetto and her wonderful son, my nephew Georgie, and his wife, Carla.

To the most important chefs in my life: Guy Savoy told this scrappy American girl it was okay to cook in his eponymous three-star Michelin joint in Paris in 1992, and it made me the cook that I am, flaws and all. My eternal thanks to Bobby Flay for his patient and unwavering guidance. Endless thanks to Guy Fieri for his support and belief in me! I can still fog a mirror. . . . Thanks to chef Geoffrey Zakarian for being one of the best chefs I have ever known.

Thanks to Brian Lando, creator of many shows, including *Alex vs. America,* the absolute best nuts-and-bolts guy I have ever known. A special thanks as well to Steve Kroopnick and John Bravakis from Triage Entertainment—you guys just love to follow me around with a camera and watch me cook great food and burn stuff. Thanks to Jesse Belodoff for being a talented friend and collaborator.

Special thanks to extraordinary publicists and dear, precious friends alike: Tara Halper, Jaret Keller, and sweet "buh bye" boy Chase.

Butter. Twenty-three years later: Chef Michael "Butter is an Italian restaurant" Jenkins, Alvaro Buchelly, the incredible Jamaal "Edward 40hands" Dunlap, Antonio "a la Morales" Morales, pastry chef extraordinaire and Halloween overlord Kevin O'Brien, Miguel "Mango" Angel Cruz, Mendoza, Flaviano "Muscle Milk" Sosa, DJSerge1 "You're fired again" Ramirez, Tony Ramirez, and many others. If you've worked at Butter, well, you've always worked at Butter then. You are also forever family . . .

Thanks to the purveyors and farmers: Pat LaFrieda, Mark Pastore and Louis Rozzo, Marilee Foster, Pike Farms, Balsam Farms, Green Thumb Organic, Amber Waves, and Quail Hill Farm. Special thanks to Daniel Zausner and Chris Studley from Levy Group.

Special thanks to my editor, Raquel Pelzel—you worked really hard on this book! Thanks to Marysarah Quinn for the stunning and unique design of the book. Thanks to Brianne Sperber for great marketing and to David Hawk in publicity.

Thanks to the photography team, including Johnny Miller, Rebecca Jurkevich, Glen Proebstel, Tommy McKiernan, and Alexei Escajeda.

Thanks to Josh Bider and Jeff Googel for scrubbing littleneck clams; and to Jon Rosen and Strand Conover for being wonderful.

Thanks to Dave Mechlowicz, Jon Steinlauf, and Sierra Gray at Food Network for their amazing support. Special thanks to Kathleen Finch and Betsy Ayala for taking a chance on me, more than once!

Thanks to Kate Fitzpatrick and Lucia Vazquez for all their expert recipe testing and hard work.

Thanks to Colleen Grapes for being an amazing friend. Thanks to a most amazing Karen "Kiki The Oracle" Mullane. Thanks to Patti "F" Jackson for being my hero. Thanks to Lee Schrager and Ricardo Restrepo for being so supportive. Thanks to Gabe Bertaccini for being an amazing confidante and Ranger game companion. Thanks to Antonia Lofaso for an early phone call (323 . . .) and Giada De Laurentiis for her friendship. Thanks to MP Styles, Jeremy and Jarhn Blutstein, and Randy Kolhoff for being great friends!

INDEX

Library of Congress Cataloging-in-Publication Data

Names: Guarnaschelli, Alex, 1969– author. | Miller, Johnny, photographer.
Title: Italian American forever : classic recipes for everything you want to eat / Alexandra Guarnaschelli ; photographs by Johnny Miller.
Identifiers: LCCN 2024000859 (print) | LCCN 2024000860 (ebook) | ISBN 9780593578001 (hardcover) | ISBN 9780593578018 (ebook)
Subjects: LGSH: Cooking, Italian. | Cooking, American.
Classification: LCC TX723.G799 2024 (print) | LCC TX723 (ebook) | DDC 641.5945—dc23/eng/20240228
LC record available at https://lccn.loc.gov/2024000859
LC ebook record available at https://lccn.loc.gov/2024000860

ISBN 978-0-593-57800-1
Signed edition ISBN 978-0-593-80050-8
Ebook ISBN 978-0-593-57801-8

Printed in China

Editor: Raquel Pelzel | Editorial assistant: Elaine Hennig
Art director and designer: Marysarah Quinn
Production editor: Terry Deal
Production manager: Philip Leung
Compositors: Merri Ann Morrell and Hannah Hunt
Production designer: Christina Self
Food stylist: Rebecca Jurkevich
Food stylist assistant: Tommy McKiernan
Prop stylist: Glen Proebstel
Prop stylist assistant: Alexei Escajeda
Copy editor: Deri Reed
Proofreaders: Hope Clarke and Tess Rossi
Indexer: Elizabeth T. Parson
Publicists: David Hawk and Natalie Yera-Campbell
Marketer: Brianne Sperber

10 9 8 7 6 5 4 3 2 1

First Edition